ROSE HEINEY

Rose Heiney is a screenwriter and novelist. Her first novel, *The Days of Judy B*, was published in 2008. Since then, she has worked primarily as a writer for television. *Elephants* is her first play.

Other Titles in this Series

Rose Heiney

ELEPHANTS

NICK HERN BOOKS

London

www.nickhernbooks.co.uk

A Nick Hern Book

Elephants first published in Great Britain in 2014 as a paperback original by Nick Hern Books Limited, The Glasshouse, 49a Goldhawk Road, London W12 8QP

Elephants copyright © 2014 Rose Heiney

Rose Heiney has asserted her moral right to be identified as the author of this work

Cover image: www.istockphoto.com/DebbiSmirnoff

Designed and typeset by Nick Hern Books, London
Printed in the UK by Mimeo Ltd, Huntingdon, Cambridgeshire PE29 6XX

A CIP catalogue record for this book is available from the British Library

ISBN 978 1 84842 439 5

Elephants was first performed at Hampstead Theatre Downstairs, London, on 11 December 2014. The cast was as follows:

VALERIE	Helen Atkinson-Wood
CHRISTOPHER	Adam Buchanan
DICK	Jonathan Guy Lewis
RICHARD	Richard Lintern
DAISY	Bel Powley
SALLY	Imogen Stubbs
LIZZY	Antonia Thomas
Director	Tamara Harvey
Designer	Polly Sullivan
Lighting	Mark Howland
Sound	Tom Gibbons

Characters

RICHARD, *mid-fifties*
SALLY, *mid-fifties*
DICK, *early fifties*
VALERIE, *early fifties*
LIZZY, *twenty-two*
DAISY, *nineteen*
CHRISTOPHER, *nineteen*

This text went to press before the end of rehearsals and so may differ slightly from the play as performed.

ACT ONE

Scene One

Christmas Eve. Living room/kitchen.

The solo at the beginning of 'Once in Royal David's City'. A gorgeous, cosy, family home – low beams, a large, beautifully decorated Christmas tree. Open fireplace. Decorations everywhere, four stockings hanging by the fire. A little carved wooden nativity scene on the mantelpiece. Picture-perfect Christmas.

There are three large-ish, framed photos on the mantelpiece. An elderly woman, a blond, good-looking nineteen-year-old boy, and a head-and-shoulders portrait of a black-and-white cat.

The living room extends into the kitchen – they're separated by a wall but we can see both. On the other side of the room, a door leading out into the porch. Adjacent to that, a door which leads upstairs.

It's dark outside.

RICHARD *is slumped in a chair in the living room. He's halfway through a bottle of red wine, and is watching telly. The news.*

NEWSREADER *(on telly)*. A nineteen-year-old man has been stabbed to death in Trafalgar Square, on one of the busiest shopping days in the capital's calendar. Twelve people have been arrested in connection with the stabbing. We'll now go live to our reporter on the scene. Kelly, can you tell us what's happening – ?

SALLY, *in an apron, comes in, carrying a portable pet cage. She's also wearing red Crocs with a white-fur trim. She puts the cage down, goes over to* RICHARD *and kisses him on the top of the head. Sees what he's watching on telly.*

REPORTER (*on telly*). Thanks, Peter. I'm here in Trafalgar Square, where Christmas revellers were shocked this afternoon when a fight broke out between what appear to have been two opposing groups of youths –

SALLY. Don't watch that.

RICHARD *turns off the telly via remote control. SALLY looks at the wine.*

I'm doing mull, you know.

RICHARD. Yes. I'm just… bracing myself for company.

SALLY. Well, I hope you're good and braced. Because I'd give them –

RICHARD *looks at his watch.*

RICHARD. Nine minutes. Six-ish, we said? 5:53 now. They'll have parked the car at the end of the drive at 5:50, and turned the headlights off so we can't see them. He'll be looking at his watch.

SALLY. Richard…

RICHARD. Yes. '5:53. We'll move off up the drive at 5:58 at a steady pace, Main House ETA, 6:02. Punctual, but not *too* punctual.'

SALLY. They're easy guests. They're on our wavelength. They'll be… perfect. And they've driven all the way from Devon so the least you can do is be nice.

RICHARD *gets up, goes over to the drinks cabinet. He puts down his wine glass and gets himself another drink – bit of whisky, bit of ginger wine.*

RICHARD. Yes. No. You're right. Perfect. Never a moment's bother from Valerie and Dick. 'Hullo, we're Valerie and Dick.' Why does he say it like that? 'Hullo.' 'H–U–L–LO.' 'Hullo.' Like a vicar in a sitcom.

RICHARD *makes a noise, a sort of small, dismissive, 'huh'.*

SALLY *approaches him with the pet basket.* RICHARD *peers into the basket, holding his drink.*

Hullo.

SALLY. I thought you might want to give Mr Biscuits a kiss.

RICHARD. Why on earth would I want to do that?

SALLY. Well, he can't come out till Boxing Day now.

RICHARD. I really don't think you're giving him enough credit.

SALLY. Kittens are easily overwhelmed by company. If we put too much pressure on him at this stage, he may never trust us again.

RICHARD. And what a terrible terrible tragedy that would be.

SALLY. It's for Daisy. We got him for Daisy.

RICHARD. Yes, when's she coming? Shouldn't she be here?

SALLY. Any minute. There was a hold-up. She emailed.

SALLY *takes her phone out of her pocket, scrolls down the find the email, and gives it to* RICHARD. *He looks at the phone. Squints.*

RICHARD. Can't read it.

SALLY. Drunk.

RICHARD. Blind! Not drunk. Old and blind. Read it to me.

SALLY *takes back the phone, and reads him the email.* RICHARD *sits down with his new drink.*

SALLY *(reading).* 'Mum. I hope that all's well with you. I've been advised to email you before departure, to let you know how things have been going. As you know, I opted for "no contact" during my stay here, as my team and I agreed that my "Family of Origin Issues" were very much the cause of my incident. I say that with no accusation whatsoever. The issues are within me, you did not cause them, you cannot control them, and you cannot cure them. They are mine and mine alone. But I wanted to get that straight. I really hope that this Christmas you, me and Dad can all detach from one another with love. Obviously we can't literally detach, as we'll be spending quite a lot of time together, enjoying the festivities. But emotionally, I hope that we can avoid becoming enmeshed – '

RICHARD. What the fuck – ?

SALLY. Just let me finish. (*Reads*.) 'I hope that we can avoid becoming enmeshed in one another's grief, whilst meeting our own needs and honouring our boundaried interconnectedness, thus avoiding the sort of behaviour which quite frankly got me into this mess in the first place. Last Christmas was obviously challenging, to say the least, and there's obviously nothing to be done about that. We must simply live compassionately through the consequences of those dark, dark days, appreciating the present and honouring the future as best we can.'

RICHARD. Who does she think she is, the Bishop of London?

SALLY (*reads*). 'I am of course ambivalent about our choosing to celebrate at all this year. But as discussed, I am going to compromise, because compromise is necessary in this life. However, I sincerely hope that this year's Christmas tree won't have a star on the top. Decorations I can live with, but the star would be a bridge too far I think. Likewise, I hope that we can focus lovingly on intimacy-slash-truth – I certainly intend-slash-hope to be able to do so. I plan on staying at home from tonight – the twenty-fourth – until the morning of the twenty-seventh at the latest. I regret that I can't stay longer, but as you know I'm undergoing an intense recovery process. This Christmas is very much a "trial period" for me within the family unit. Whilst I'm optimistic about the outcome, I must stay connected to my team and my support systems here. As such, I may – if, and *only if* absolutely necessary – spend a certain amount of time on the phone to Lynda – '

RICHARD. Oh, Lynda! Of *course*! Dear Lynda!

SALLY. ' – to Lynda, my primary contact at the centre. Please don't be offended by this. And please don't be offended by my arriving a little later than I said I would tonight, probably about 6:15 if my taxi driver does his job properly. I felt that it would be wise for me to complete a further boundary-setting exercise here before I'm let loose in front of Valerie and Dick. Finally, this: if we refer to my incident and the weeks leading up to my incident at all during the festive period, I'd appreciate it if we could avoid the term "nervous breakdown". I am in the early stages of choosing to see it more as a positive forwards transformation in my life, and such damning and perjorative language is unhelpful to me on my journey. Please respect that. Happy Christmas, Mum. I love you. I can't wait to meet Mr Biscuits.' Then 'Daisy', and three kisses.

SALLY *puts the phone in her pocket.* RICHARD *slumps back in his chair.*

RICHARD. Christ. For twenty grand you'd think they'd have made her a bit nicer.

SALLY. Don't make this harder than it needs to be.

RICHARD. Harder than it needs to be? You know, I think you're insane. For trying to do this. Completely insane. We could have gone to the Caribbean. Gone to New York, stayed at The Plaza –

SALLY. We always said, Christmas isn't Christmas if it's in a hotel –

RICHARD. Well, we could have dug a hole, then, and curled up in it with a barrel of gin! Anything! Anything but this – this – murders on the news –

SALLY. I said don't watch it.

RICHARD. – and all the old baubles out and bloody – bloody – (*Hissing.*) *Valerie and Dick* banging on about their gay daughter and how 'absolutely lovely and fine' they are about it –

SALLY. They won't bang on! And Christmas is important, Richard. We agreed –

RICHARD. You agreed.

SALLY. – that we'd make a decent fist of it this year. We deserve it. We deserve our Christmas. And I've been working for two days straight sorting the presents and –

RICHARD *gets up – leaving his glass behind – and makes a move towards the front door (offstage).*

– making sure everyone can get here and getting the good crackers and making the stuffing and shelling so many nuts that *my knuckles are bleeding, Richard –*

SALLY *shows* RICHARD *a plaster on her knuckle.*

RICHARD. All right! Understood! Understood. Christ. Where's my coat? What have you done with it? (*Accusatory, suspicious.*) Have you done something *festive* with it?

SALLY. It's upstairs. Where are you going?

RICHARD. I need a fag.

SALLY. You can't have one. There's no time. It's not fair to Valerie and Dick –

RICHARD. Oh, yes, *heaven forbid* that Valerie and Dick should be momentarily uncomfortable! Roll out the red carpet, raise the flag for *Valerie and Dick –*

The doorbell rings. SALLY *goes off to answer it. It's* VALERIE *and* DICK. RICHARD *slumps back in his chair and listens to the greetings.*

SALLY (*offstage*). Valerie! Dick!

DICK (*offstage*). Hullo!

VALERIE (*offstage*). Happy / Christmas!

DICK (*offstage*). Happy Christmas!

Kisses and handshakes all round. Removing of coats, etc.

SALLY (*offstage*). Let me take your / things.

VALERIE (*offstage*). Thank you.

SALLY *slings their coats over her arm, and re-enters with* VALERIE *and* DICK *close behind her. They're a smiling couple in their early fifties, with overnight bags and bags of presents.*

SALLY. We're putting coats upstairs. I hope no one minds, I thought it might be festive. Bit of a 'house party' vibe, ha ha! Except Richard's coat, obviously, we'll have to have that by the door, in case he needs to go out to –

DICK. Smoke! Oh yes? Still on the fags, Richard?

VALERIE *shoots* DICK *a bit of a look.*

SALLY. He's giving up.

VALERIE. Gosh, are you? Well done, Richard, that's very impressive.

RICHARD *raises his glass.*

RICHARD. Yes, I kept setting fire to my tumbler of meths. Eyebrows – (*Mimes a small 'explosion'.*) Treacherous.

VALERIE *and* DICK *see* RICHARD*'s drink. Exchange a quick glance.*

DICK. I heard that giving up smoking's harder than giving up heroin.

SALLY. Well, we wouldn't know anything about that.

DICK. No, no, it is. Smoking is one of the most intricate and terrifying traps that man and nature have ever conspired to create. Did you know that the physiological effects of smoking take –

The kitten mewls from the portable cage.

– up to seven years to fully leave your / system.

RICHARD. Is that right? Is it really? Is that right, Dick? That's wonderful.

VALERIE. What was that?

SALLY *holds up the cage. Another mewling noise.*

SALLY. Oh, this is Mr Biscuits! The newest member of our clan. He's locked up till Boxing Day, I'm afraid. But do take a peek.

VALERIE *and* DICK *peer into the cage. A louder meow, and a hissing noise. They rear back in shock.*

I know. He's nervous. Aren't you, Mr Biscuits? Aren't you a little ball of worry? It's normal. He's only little.

VALERIE. Maybe if we stroked him –

SALLY. No, that makes him angry.

VALERIE. Oh.

SALLY. He's for Daisy, really.

VALERIE. Oh, where is she? Lovely Daisy.

SALLY. She's on her way back now. She went away for a little rest after term.

RICHARD. Mm. Knackering, these modern unversities. Lectures up to four hours a week, I've heard. Shouldn't be allowed.

DICK. Is she off Club Eighteen-to-Thirty-ing? Binge-boozing in Malaga? I read an article –

SALLY. Yes, speaking of which – shall we get the drinks up and running? Who's for mull? (*Hands the coats to* RICHARD, *who accepts them reluctantly.*) You put the coats in the special place, I'll wrangle the drinks.

Make yourselves at home.

SALLY *goes into the kitchen.* RICHARD *goes upstairs with the coats.*

VALERIE *and* DICK *hover in the living room. They seem uncomfortable.* DICK *goes over to the mantelpiece, and stares at the photo of the nineteen-year-old boy.*

VALERIE. Don't stare.

DICK. Well, they put it there.

VALERIE. That doesn't mean you need to stare at it. Just treat it like a birthmark. It's there, and everyone knows it's there, but that doesn't mean it needs talking about.

DICK. But are we mentioning it, or not mentioning it?

VALERIE. Well, probably a bit of both. We follow their lead.

DICK. They should have told us in advance. Mentioning or not mentioning. We could have prepared.

VALERIE. It's not up to us. If they want to talk about it, they'll make it clear.

DICK *sighs. Moment of silence.*

DICK. I don't like that kitten.

VALERIE. You've not met him properly.

DICK. Still, I don't like him. He's a bad thing, I can tell.

VALERIE. He's a kitten! Maybe Richard and Sally just need something new to love –

RICHARD *comes downstairs.*

RICHARD. Is this the kitten? Yes, we're all going to hate him. Dreadful thing. Sitting there squalling and making the whole house smell of piss. (*Points at the photograph of the cat on the mantelpiece.*) That one – rivers of piss. Decades and decades of passive aggression and purring and a fucking Niagara Falls of piss. Miserable. Can't stand the bloody things. Where's the mull? (*Calls into kitchen.*) *Sally!*

RICHARD *picks up his whisky and ginger wine from before. Drains it.*

VALERIE *clocks the four stockings hanging in front of the fireplace.*

VALERIE. Will it just be us and Daisy?

RICHARD. No, there's someone else. Did you ever meet Lizzy? She's – (*Calls in to the kitchen.*) Sally, how do you explain Lizzy?

SALLY *comes in with a tray – four glasses of mulled wine and some mince pies. As she speaks,* RICHARD, VALERIE *and* DICK *take their glasses, and a mince pie.*

SALLY. Oh, Lizzy's wonderful! You must have met her. From City Mates – the charity which Christopher was on his way to when –

VALERIE. Mm.

SALLY. He was –

DICK. Mm –

SALLY. – yes. She always used to come for summers and Christmases and things.

VALERIE. Oh hold, on – we did meet her! Of course. City Mates Lizzy – tracksuit-and-trainers Lizzy. Suffolk Show, 2004. She must have been about twelve –

SALLY. Mm. I mean, she's from an awful background, but she's a lovely girl. Lives up a tower in Peckham, like Rapunzel, ha! And she's shimmied down the golden rope to come and eat sprouts with us. We thought –

RICHARD. *You* thought.

SALLY. – it would be nice to have someone here who knew Christopher. Knew him outside the family, I mean. Obviously –

DICK *looks at* VALERIE. *Clearly they are 'talking about it'.* VALERIE *nods back. Game on.*

– we've all got our own memories, but she knew him as an… individual adult human.

DICK. Very well put.

SALLY. They became sort of –

RICHARD. '*Lovers.*'

SALLY. Close. Briefly close. Nothing serious. Just, you know, late teens. Spent some summers together. Larky fun, you know, the young, ha!

VALERIE. Did we meet her at the –

RICHARD. Funeral? No, she didn't come.

SALLY. She works. She's done very well for herself. Ever so busy, we had a hell of a job persuading her to come down –

RICHARD. Ha! Sally hounded her for months. (*Mimicking SALLY.*) 'Hel-lo, Lizzy! It's Sally Llewellyn! Just to say that I know I've already called you twice this morning and I know it's only September but I'm out buying crackers and was just wondering what your favourite sort of cracker was! That is, if you are coming for Christmas, ha / ha ha – '

SALLY. She's *thrilled* to be coming. And it'll be wonderful for us to have the younger generation out in force. Fresh blood, you know?

VALERIE. Lovely for Daisy.

SALLY. Mm. And Lizzy's part of the family, really. A second daughter. I mean – ha – Daisy's plenty –

RICHARD. Plenty.

SALLY. – but… gain through loss. Anyway, she's coming and it's going to be wonderful for us all to see her.

VALERIE. Well, that sounds lovely. Oh dear, we haven't bought her a present, I'm afraid.

SALLY. Oh, that's all covered. I got her and Daisy a pair of tickets to see – what's-his-name, I found him on the internet – Professor Green. He's a rapper. I thought they could go together in the new year. And I got them vouchers so they can have Nando's together afterwards.

DICK. Cor. That sounds like a… cracking night out.

SALLY. Well, it might not be to your taste. But we have to honour the young.

VALERIE. Absolutèly. Good for you.

Quick pause. They sip their drinks.

SALLY. How's Jennifer? How's Sydney?

VALERIE. Oh, absolutely / lovely.

DICK. Fine.

SALLY. Are they married yet? Her and – ?

RICHARD. Is it marriage? When they're both –

SALLY. Yes, it is.

RICHARD. But is it *marriage*-marriage? In Australia?

SALLY. Yes, Richard, it is.

VALERIE. Sherelle.

DICK. Not yet. Some time in the new year.

SALLY. Great.

RICHARD. Lovely.

VALERIE. We're very much looking forward to it.

SALLY. It must be hard. First Christmas without her.

VALERIE. Yes – well. I mean, it's nothing compared to / your –

SALLY. Oh, no, we won't be having any of that! Missing people isn't a competition, you know. We're all very much in the same boat.

VALERIE. Well, quite. That's very generous of you, Sally.

SALLY. Not a problem.

A lull.

SALLY *playfully sticks out her foot – shows* VALERIE *and* DICK *her Crocs.*

Does anyone recognise these?

VALERIE. Oh my goodness – are they – ?

DICK. The Christmas Crocs!

SALLY. I know. The Christopher Crocs. The first present he
ever bought me. It's a rite of passage, isn't it? The first time
your child spends money on you.

RICHARD. A sound payback for ninety grand in school fees.

SALLY. It was a lovely gesture.

RICHARD. They make your feet look like beans.

VALERIE. Well, I think they're wonderful.

*An awkward pause. Everybody takes a sip of their mulled
wine.* SALLY *indicates the decorations.*

SALLY. I've pulled out all the stops.

DICK. So I see.

SALLY. I mean, why not?

VALERIE. Absolutely.

SALLY. I had this overwhelming *urge*, you know, to do things
beautifully. Obviously, we don't want to put too much
pressure on ourselves –

VALERIE. No.

SALLY. – but we have to honour it. We have to honour him.
And the wonderful thing about Christmas is it's sort of in a
bubble, isn't it? No news –

DICK. Apart from that poor boy in Traf–

VALERIE (*silencing*). Dick.

DICK. No, no news. Literally absolutely nothing happening.

SALLY. We all turn our phones off, and it's just us, people we
love, and memories of people we love. I've done a
marvellous thing, look – (*Indicating a string of dried orange
peel on the mantelpiece, above the nativity scene.*) I
squeezed out some oranges, put the turkey in the juice to

soak, then dried the oranges out in the airing cupboard and strung them up with cinnamon and draped them round the crib. And all the food's organic. Everything. Apart from the cinnamon, but I don't know if you can get that organic.

VALERIE *looks. It's a bit weird.*

VALERIE. Gosh, that's… stunning. Really lovely, Sally.

SALLY. Well, there's no reason why it shouldn't be lovely.

VALERIE. No.

SALLY. Everybody expects us to be horribly *damaged*, don't they? Wounded. So it's up to us to show them that we're not. We're still here. We're still ourselves. We're not broken, we're not *less than*. I've done the flowerbed as well, just how he would have wanted it, snowdrops. They're a bit droopy but still rather fine I think. So yes, there's sadness. But still heaps of room for jollity.

VALERIE. Yes. Absolutely. I look forward to it.

DICK. A very Merry Christmas to us all!

RICHARD*'s not enjoying his mulled wine.*

RICHARD. There's something terribly wrong with this.

SALLY. It's non-alcoholic.

RICHARD *spits a mouthful of wine back into his glass.*

RICHARD. What? Are you trying to poison us?

SALLY (*to* VALERIE *and* DICK). I've not had a drink for nine months. It's the longest I've gone since I was pregnant with Christopher –

RICHARD. She drank all through Daisy. Like Oliver Reed, she was. Caning her way round the NCT classes.

SALLY. I was not. No, I thought – 'Sally,' I thought – 'this is hard enough. And drink might appear to be making it easier, but is it? Is it really? No.' So now, whenever I think I want a drink, I go upstairs and kick all the pillows until it passes.

DICK. Oh.

SALLY. And our lives are much better for it, aren't they, Richard?

RICHARD *is pouring whisky into his mulled wine.*

RICHARD. Mm.

SALLY. That's your ninth unit.

RICHARD. What?

SALLY. Your ninth. Six in the half-bottle of wine, two in the whisky mac. You're keeping it to eight units a day, remember? And it's only six o'clock.

RICHARD. I've gone into Christmas units.

SALLY. The first day of Christmas is tomorrow. You can go into Christmas units tomorrow.

RICHARD. Oh, can I? How kind. Well, I'll have you know I've been in Christmas units since / October.

DICK. What's the recommended units? It's eighteen to twenty-five, isn't it?

VALERIE. No, that's body mass index.

SALLY. Richard's been sticking to eight. I started keeping a log –

RICHARD. A spreadsheet. An Excel spreadsheet.

SALLY. All right, yes, a spreadsheet of his drinks, and it averaged out at eight units a night in order to stay festive. Any more than that and he tips over into maudlin. So we agreed, eight.

RICHARD. Well, I'm very firmly in Christmas units. And I plan to stay in Christmas units until the fifth, when I imagine I'll go in to crisis units because of the trial –

SALLY. We're not talking about the trial –

DICK *glances at* VALERIE, *worried. Talking about it, or not talking about it?*

RICHARD. Then I'll be needing my units to shut me up, won't I?

RICHARD *raises his glass, defiant. Drinks.*

Pause.

VALERIE (*polite*). You never did say where Daisy's been.

RICHARD (*clearing his throat*). She's –

The doorbell rings.

SALLY. – here! She's here!

SALLY *puts the tray down and goes over to the door. Opens it.* LIZZY – *black, well-dressed, beautifully made up and wearing very high heels – is standing there, again with an overnight bag and a bag of presents. She's friendly, eager, maybe a bit nervous.*

Lizzy!

LIZZY. Happy Christmas!

LIZZY *gives* SALLY *a hug.*

SALLY. Happy Christmas! Lizzy, this is Valerie and Dick, Valerie and Dick, this is Lizzy, from City Mates, Daisy's friend. And you know Richard of course.

LIZZY. I do. Hi, Richard.

She goes over and gives RICHARD *a kiss.*

RICHARD (*a bit chilly*). Hello, Lizzy. Good of you to come.

LIZZY. Oh, no, thanks for having me. I've been really looking forward to it.

RICHARD. Have you?

SALLY. Let me take your things – we're putting the coats upstairs, more party-ish, we thought –

SALLY *takes* LIZZY*'s things.*

RICHARD. Mm, a hoot.

SALLY (*ignores him, speaks to* LIZZY). Would you like some mulled wine?

RICHARD. It's non-alcoholic.

VALERIE. It's lovely.

SALLY. And can I take your presents? (*Takes the bag and peers into it.*) Oh, they are beautifully wrapped, you're putting us all to shame.

LIZZY. Oh, it's not much, just bit and bobs. Um – I – I don't mean to scare you but I think there's someone in the bushes.

SALLY. What?

LIZZY. I mean – I'm not sure. It could have been a fox or something. But it looked a lot like a person.

SALLY. Richard, could you go and –

RICHARD. Yes, fine! Send me off into the arms of the axe-man. She's like Field Marshal Haig. Still, at least there'll be a fag in it for me.

RICHARD *takes his coat and goes outside.* SALLY *calls after him.*

SALLY. Don't let the smoke blow in through the –

RICHARD *slams the door behind him.*

– door. I'll get your drink, Lizzy.

LIZZY. Thank you.

LIZZY *smiles awkwardly at* VALERIE *and* DICK. DICK *is mesmerised by* LIZZY.

DICK. You look like a supermodel.

VALERIE. Dick! (*To* LIZZY.) Don't mind him.

LIZZY. Don't worry. Thank you, Dick, that's very sweet of you.

DICK *pretty much giggles with delight. Awkward pause.*

VALERIE *and* DICK *speak simultaneously.*

VALERIE / DICK. How was your journey? / Did you know their son well?

VALERIE *shoots* DICK *a look.*

DICK. What? I thought we were talking about it!

LIZZY. My journey was fine, thank you. And yes, quite well.

VALERIE. It's so sad. I'm sure it's really nice for them to have you here.

LIZZY. Yeah, it's lovely of them to ask. I wasn't sure, I mean – it's weird, isn't it? But Sally seemed really keen for me to come.

DICK. Did you know that boy? The boy on the news from Trafalgar Square?

VALERIE *turns on* DICK.

VALERIE. Now, why would she have known him? Why would you say that? Sorry, Lizzy. We live in a barn. We breed horses. Dick's not been to London since the eighties, and that was just for *Phantom of the Opera.* He doesn't mean any harm –

DICK. I was only asking –

LIZZY (*laughing*). It's fine. No, I didn't know him.

DICK. Do you know people who knew him? You must know –

VALERIE. Dick, stop it.

DICK. – some people. Is it gangs, do you think? Now, I'll tell you a thing about gangs. When the horses don't get fed for a while, what they tend to do is huddle together in a corner of the field. In what you could call a 'gang'. Now, if you were to place a rival 'gang' of better-fed horses in an adjacent field –

VALERIE. Dick!

DICK *stops talking.*

(*To* LIZZY.) I hear that you and Daisy are great pals.

LIZZY*'s not quite sure how to respond.*

LIZZY. Well –

She's interrupted by RICHARD*'s re-entry.* RICHARD *is pulling a wheeled suitcase.*

RICHARD. It was Father Christmas himself! He bought the presents in a wheelie-case.

He's followed into the room by DAISY. *Bare-faced and wearing a tracksuit with a hooded top. She's on edge, defensive.*

VALERIE. Daisy! Wonderful to see you. Happy Christmas!

DAISY. I've not bought any presents.

DICK. Not even an airport Toblerone? Bottle of Scotch for your old da– for... anyone? No, bet you drank it on the party bus, you little scamp. (*Sings.*) *Agadoo-doo-doo! Push pineapple shake a tree* – (*Picks up on the atmosphere, peters out.*)

DAISY (*to* RICHARD, *quietly*). Where does he think I've been?

LIZZY *smiles.*

LIZZY. Hi, Daisy.

DAISY. Oh fuck, it's you.

DAISY *turns on her heel and heads out of the door again.* RICHARD *grabs her by the scruff of the neck.*

RICHARD. No you don't, missy. You've spent quite enough time in the bushes.

DAISY. I couldn't come in. I experienced a block. (*Looks at* LIZZY.) What's she doing here?

RICHARD. She's come for Christmas.

DAISY. She's bloody not.

RICHARD. She has, I'm afraid.

DICK *turns to* LIZZY, *conspiratorial.*

DICK. What's got into her, eh?

LIZZY *doesn't respond. She's looking at* DAISY.

LIZZY. Your mum invited me. She thought it would be fun.

DAISY. No – why is she here? This is the – how *could* she, I mean – this is –

LIZZY. Daisy, I –

DAISY *holds her hand up.*

DAISY. *No!*

DAISY *stops talking and turns to face the door. Talks to herself, still audible to the others.*

One-two-three-CALM-two-three-one-two-three-CALM-two-three –

SALLY *comes back into the room with a glass of mulled wine and a plate of pigs in blankets.*

SALLY. Lizzy, I've put you in the Little Room – Daisy! My little Daisy-bell! Happy Christmas!

SALLY *puts down the glass and the drinks, and goes over to give* DAISY *a hug.* DAISY*'s still got her back turned, still muttering.*

DAISY. One-two-three-CALM-two-three –

SALLY. Daisy? Sweetheart?

DAISY. DONE. (*Turns round and addresses her mother.*) Hi, Mum. Happy Christmas!

SALLY. Happy Christmas, darling.

SALLY *looks quizzically at* RICHARD *over* DAISY*'s shoulder.* RICHARD *shrugs.*

Oh, we're all here. It's every mother's dream. Daisy, would you like a drink?

DAISY. No thanks. I'm not drinking this Christmas. Alcohol erects a wall between me and my feelings. And I'm choosing to feel my feelings. Sorry.

RICHARD. It's non-alcoholic.

He's pouring himself a large whisky.

SALLY. Well, if we're all here and happy, how about we light the Christmas candles?

RICHARD. We're having a ceremony.

VALERIE. Oh, that's lovely.

RICHARD. Yes, it is, isn't it? We've been rehearsing since Tuesday. Unfortunately the band of the Royal Marines was unavailable.

SALLY *places three candles on the mantelpiece. One in front of the picture of the nineteen-year-old boy, one in front of the old lady, and one in front of the cat.*

RICHARD, DAISY, VALERIE, DICK *and* LIZZY *look on formally.* SALLY *holds up a taper. She's got nothing to light it with.*

SALLY. Has anyone got a – ?

RICHARD *produces a cigarette lighter from his pocket.* SALLY *takes it from him, with a look. Lights the taper.*

And could you dim the lights.

RICHARD *dims the lights.*

Good. Music? No. (*She's stalling.*) Should we hold hands? How would everyone feel about holding hands?

RICHARD. Just light the bloody things.

SALLY *pulls a piece of paper out of her pocket. Clears her throat.*

SALLY. Okay. As you all know, this Christmas is very much about loss. And we're honoured and humbled that Valerie, Dick and Lizzy chose to be here to share it with us. So I saw fit to –

RICHARD. For God's sake, woman, you're not opening a leisure centre.

SALLY. So I saw fit to commission a little poem from a very talented young man, Jason 'Jase' Ademola. Jase – as you may know, Lizzy –

LIZZY *smiles awkwardly.*

– is a beneficiary of City Mates, a charity our late son, and Daisy's late brother –

DAISY *puts a hand to her mouth. She's going to be sick. Swallows it.*

DAISY. I'm fine.

SALLY. – Christopher, was closely associated with. And I thought we'd use his words tonight to honour our fallen.

VALERIE. Lovely.

SALLY. Thank you.

SALLY *puts a candle in front of the old lady picture.*

Grandma Wilson.

RICHARD *mutters to* DICK.

RICHARD. Sally's mother. Died 2009. Congestive heart failure, and a bad attitude.

DICK. Ah.

SALLY (*reads*).
    'Gone but not forgotten. May all our dead live on in our
      hearts
    Until the last of us is extinguished
    And the last of our souls joins with theirs
    In the everafter. We loved them. God bless them, and God
      bless our love and all who shared it.'

SALLY *lights the candle.*

RICHARD. That doesn't rhyme.

RICHARD*'s drunk.*

SALLY *moves over to the photo of the nineteen-year-old boy.*

SALLY. Christopher James Llewellyn.

(*Reads*.)

    'Gone but not forgotten. May all our dead live on in our hearts

    Until the last of us is extinguished

    And the last of our souls joins with theirs

    In the everafter. We loved them. God bless them, and God bless our love and all who shared it.'

SALLY *lights the candle*.

Quite a long pause.

SALLY *moves over to the picture of the cat*.

Buttons Llewellyn.

RICHARD. Oh, for fuck's sake.

SALLY (*reads*).

    'Gone but not forgotten. May all our dead live on in our hearts

    Until the last of us is extinguished

    And the last of our souls joins with theirs

    In the everafter. We loved them. God bless them, and God bless our love and all who shared it.'

SALLY *lights the candle*.

A long pause. Nobody quite knows what to do. SALLY *chuckles*.

I feel as if someone ought to say 'Amen'.

DICK. Amen.

RICHARD *turns the lights up*.

SALLY. Dinner's at eight. (*To* RICHARD.) And you – go and have a nap in the shed.

Scene Two

Richard's shed.

RICHARD, *alone, in his shed in the garden. It's a bit of a tip –
a lone armchair, a small telly, and cardboard boxes and boxes
of tools. Lit only by a small lamp, and the flickering of his telly.
He's slumped in an armchair, feet up on a cardboard box. He's
got a fag on the go, and is swigging red wine straight from the
bottle. He's also intermittently spooning coffee granules into his
mouth direct from the jar.*

He's watching the news.

REPORTER (*on telly*). 'The Metropolitan Police are feeding us
more information about the fatal stabbing in Trafalgar
Square we were telling you about a short time ago. Police
say that they were called to the scene at about 13:45 to
reports of a male stabbed in Trafalgar Square, central
London. Now, they're saying that the location of the incident
was just metres south of the square's large Christmas tree, no
doubt surrounded by Christmas Eve revellers. Police were
straight away on the scene, and it's believed that a young
man was pronounced dead at around 14:00 hours today.
Twelve arrests have been made, and police are appealing for
any information on the incident. We'll bring you more on
this of course as further details reach us…'

RICHARD *spoons more coffee granules into his mouth.
Washes them down with wine. Stares at the telly.*

Living room.

A trestle table has been set up in the living room; VALERIE
is laying the table. SALLY *is in the kitchen (offstage)
preparing dinner. Putting handfuls of sprouts into a blender,
pulverising them, then putting the pulverised sprouts into a
sauté pan to cook. She wanders in and out during the
following scene, as she chats with* VALERIE.

VALERIE. I think it's great that you're doing this.

SALLY. Well, I've boiled them ten years on the trot, and just
sort of dumped them next to the turkey. So I thought this

year; Jamie Oliver, and we'll have them on Christmas Eve. I mean, they might as well be cabbage to be honest, but you've got to ring the changes.

VALERIE. No, I mean… Christmas. The full… so soon after –

SALLY. Yes. (*Quickly.*) Well, it has to be done, doesn't it? I realised, straight away – and I'm sticking to this – that there'll always be a hole –

Blast on the blender. SALLY *removes the sprouts. Puts more in.*

VALERIE. Mm.

SALLY. – *there'll always be a hole.* But what you have to do is – fill the hole with positives. Just fill it up, stuff it like a stocking. And I really feel we've done that. The Foundation. The poetry. Lizzy. All positives.

VALERIE. Absolutely. I don't know how you've / done it.

SALLY. Well, we have. And we stay *open.* We talk about *everything.* I find myself – still, I mean – talking to strangers in the shop. Discussing the mechanics of a stab wound over the Battenbergs. (*Laughs.*) You have to, don't you? (*Quick blast on the blender.*) You have to go in and say 'this is me. This is my life. This is an incontrovertible fact about my life. And you may find it – ha – repellent, or shocking, or "a bit much" – but it isn't. It's just a fact.' Fact. (*Another blast on the blender.*) Like Jennifer.

VALERIE. That's – not quite the / same.

SALLY. No, but it's still hard, isn't it? Her on the other side of the world. Living – well, it can't be what you imagined.

SALLY*'s gathering another handful of sprouts.*

VALERIE. No, but –

SALLY. How's Dick doing?

VALERIE. Oh, he's coming round. Heaving himself into the twenty-first century. Two steps forward, one step back. You know.

SALLY. Mm. Well, it's wonderful we've got each other. For
Christmas. We're all so happy you could come. It's perfect.
All of us together, none of us quite right, none of us having
to pretend anything to anyone. It's exactly as it should be.

VALERIE *nods*.

Because you *have* to be able to tell anyone *anything*. Don't
you? Whether or not they think they want to hear it. No
secrets. Blood and guts? Pfft! Just say it! *Everyone's got
them, you know.*

SALLY *wanders in from the kitchen with a large knife in her
hand*.

I'll just say to people, I'll just go up to them and say – my
son's abdominal wall was punctured by a six-inch blade,
between nine and fourteen times; his kidneys, intestines and
spleen were reduced, effectively, to mince. And he bled to
death on the pavement. And that's that.

She goes back into the kitchen. A blast on the blender.

VALERIE. Mm.

SALLY. What's more, this happened to him because he tried to
take a positive action. He tried to help some people who he
believed were in need, on the way to an interview which
would have enabled him to spend a whole *year* helping
people in even *greater* need. That's what happened. And it's
nothing to be ashamed of.

VALERIE. God, no. Quite the opposite.

SALLY. Well, exactly. He died a hero. And how many mothers
can say that about their sons? He died a hero. A six-page
spread in the local paper. With the headline. 'Hero.' Just one
word. 'Hero.'

VALERIE. You said. I remember.

SALLY. Good. You would, wouldn't you? Even if you *didn't*
know us. You'd remember that. 'Hero.' (*Another blast on the
blender.*)

VALERIE *nods*.

(*Laughing*.) And why – I mean, seriously, tell me – why would we deny ourselves a turkey, because our son died a hero? Why would we do that? Who'd do that? We deserve *extra* turkey. And goose-fat roast potatoes.

VALERIE. And Jamie Oliver sprouts.

Another blast on the blender.

SALLY. Quite. And all the old traditions – we'll do stockings in the morning. I've done Lizzy a wonderful stocking. (*Laughs*.) I went bananas in Superdrug. Make-up. I just went in and said to them 'I've got a girl coming for Christmas, and I want her to feel like a *princess*.'

VALERIE. How long was she with –

SALLY. Christopher? Oh, months. Four months. Just a little thing, summer thing, just after his A levels. They broke up, he thought he might want to go travelling. But she was good for him, you know? Widened his circle. It's so easy for us to get a bit – narrow, here. Yacht club. Tennis. Jack Wills, ha! She showed him a bit of life. And I'm glad of that.

VALERIE. Absolutely.

SALLY. She was shy about coming. She didn't want to intrude. But I told her, I said, you're family. You're family now, and as long as I'm alive and breathing there'll always be a paper hat and a cracker for *you*, young lady.

SALLY *pulverises some sprouts*.

VALERIE. How's the Foundation?

SALLY. Oh, coming together. The website's gone live. One of the kids from City Mates – you know, the charity which Christopher –

VALERIE. Yes.

SALLY. Yes, well. He's done the website. I'm not absolutely sure about it, to be honest, but he's a good kid – Kwame, his family's Nigerian – and he's done some lovely – what are they called? Graphics. No, that's computer games. Anyway, it looks nice. And some boys from Christopher's old school are swimming to Belgium to raise money –

VALERIE. Swimming to Belgium?

SALLY. Well, they're doing it in a pool. So the number of lengths equivalent to the distance between Harwich and Oostende, if you see what I mean –

VALERIE. I do.

SALLY. So. It's go go go.

VALERIE. You've done it so fast. Just a year –

SALLY. One year and one day.

VALERIE. Mm.

SALLY *shrugs*.

SALLY. It's for Christopher. Obviously – others will benefit, but – it's… for him.

SALLY*'s suddenly about to cry.*

VALERIE. It's – it's a privilege to be here, Sally. It really is.

SALLY. Well. He was a good boy. And it's up to us to be good too. Everybody's got to be good.

VALERIE *nods. A beat.*

SALLY *puts some sprouts in the blender.* VALERIE *carries on laying the table.*

Living room. A bit later.

The table's now laid. DAISY *and* DICK *are doing the table decorations – finishing touches, crackers, etc.*

LIZZY *is sitting in an armchair, reading* Vogue *and drinking mulled wine.*

DAISY*'s getting some wine glasses from the cupboard.*

The kitten cage is up on the sideboard.

DICK *is laying out side plates. He's laid out six – one for each place – and is about to put the remaining one back on the sideboard.*

DAISY. No, we need seven.

DICK. Why? There's six of us.

DAISY. We have to lay an extra place. For absent friends. Or Jesus. I can't remember. But one Christmas when we didn't Mum dropped the roast potatoes on Dad's foot and he had to go to hospital. So now, we set an extra place.

DICK. Oh.

DICK *lays the extra place.* DAISY *puts a wine glass in front of it. Bit of awkward contact between them. Shuffling around each other, etc.*

DAISY *grabs some holly from the sideboard and puts it in a wine glass.*

DAISY. That's to show that it's symbolic. Like, no one's going to actually sit at it.

DICK. Do you know what might be fun? If we got one of those old Resusci Anne dolls, and sat it there. Maybe put a Father Christmas hat on it. Could be jolly. Lizzy, what do you think?

LIZZY. Yeah, that might be –

DAISY. No. I wouldn't find that jolly.

DICK. Oh.

DAISY *surveys the table.*

DAISY. This isn't pretty enough. We need to make it prettier.

LIZZY *looks up from her magazine.*

LIZZY. Can I help at all?

DAISY. No, no. You just sit there like the massive great princess you are. That's what Mum used to call her, Dick. Princess Elizabeth. Do you think she looks like a princess?

DICK. She most certainly does.

DAISY. No she doesn't. Mum only said it to make her feel better because she was poor. Still, she's here now and we might as well make the best of it.

DAISY *puts a wine glass by each place.*

LIZZY. Daisy, I didn't mean to / cause any –

DAISY. I think it's best if you don't say anything, Lizzy. Mm?

LIZZY. Your mum said you wanted me here.

DAISY. She says a lot of things. And a lot of them are bollocks. Isn't that right?

LIZZY *stares at the floor.*

DICK. You two had a bit of a falling out, then?

DAISY. No. Far from it.

DICK. Oh.

DAISY. And even if we had, I wouldn't *dare* mention it. Because it's Christmas, isn't it? And everything's got to be lovely at Christmas.

DICK. Oh. Right. Jolly good.

DICK *gets some crackers from the sideboard, and starts to put one in front of each place.*

DAISY *snatches the crackers from his hand. Angry.*

DAISY. No! Crackers are for tomorrow. You can't have crackers on Christmas Eve. It's bad luck.

DAISY *takes the crackers back, and puts them on the sideboard. She then goes to each spot on the dining table where a cracker was placed, vigorously dusts it off and blows on it. She then quietly snaps the fingers of each hand three times, and looks up at the ceiling.*

DICK *can't help but stare.*

I know you think I'm odd.

DICK. Not at all.

DAISY. But I don't care. I don't bend over backwards to please people any more.

DICK. That's good, that's very good.

DAISY. I've learnt the importance of authenticity. Being whoever it is you need to be, at any given moment.

DICK. 'To thine own self be true!'

DAISY. No, not like that.

DICK. Oh.

> DAISY *goes over to the sideboard and gets out some water glasses.* DICK *looks on, a bit of a spare part.*

> *He goes over to the kitten cage. Peers in. The kitten lets out a mewl and a hiss.* DICK *shrinks back.*

> Christ.

> DAISY *puts the water glasses out while she talks.*

DAISY. I do affirmations every morning. I stand in front of the mirror, and I say 'Everything I see, I love and accept unconditionally.' And then I sit on three cushions and meditate.

> *She's getting a bit intense now.* DICK *wants to leave.*

DICK. Lizzy, how's your mull? Do you need a / top-up.

LIZZY. No, I'm fine thank you.

DAISY. In my meditation, I think of three people. First, someone I love. Like Buttons, and hopefully Mr Biscuits once I get to know him. Then someone who I don't really care about either way, like Nick Clegg or Jessica Alba or the postman. Then I think of someone I really really *hate* –

> DAISY *slams a water glass down for emphasis.* LIZZY *jumps.* DAISY *glances briefly at her.*

DICK. Oh.

DAISY. – and I say 'May they be well. May they be happy. May they be free from suffering.'

DICK. And are they?

DAISY. What?

DICK. Well and happy and… what you said.

DAISY. I don't know. When I've finished I let go.

DICK. Let go of what?

DAISY. Suffering. My suffering. Their suffering. Suffering in general.

DICK. Goodness.

DAISY. Could you pass the holly?

DICK *passes* DAISY *the holly.* DAISY *snatches it off him.*

Thank you.

She looks at the holly, and at the table, worried. She's about to make a centrepiece.

What I'd really like to do is put it in some water with some cranberries. And some glitter. (*Calls into the kitchen.*) Mum! Have we got any cranberries? *Mum?*

DAISY *goes off into the kitchen.* DICK *is alone with* LIZZY.

DICK. She's a bit moody, isn't she?

LIZZY *smiles awkwardly.*

LIZZY. Well, it's probably very hard for them. Christmas. Anniversary. All that.

DICK. Still. No need to take it out on poor old you.

LIZZY. I'll be okay.

DICK *wanders over, stands behind* LIZZY.

DICK. What are you reading?

LIZZY. *Vogue.*

She shows him the magazine.

It's like *Horse and Hound*, but with humans.

DICK *takes a moment to understand this, then laughs uproariously.*

DICK. Oh! Ha ha. Very good.

LIZZY *smiles.*

You a fan of clothes, then?

LIZZY. Yeah. I'm a fashion PR.

DICK. I thought you worked for – what is it – the charity. City Mates.

LIZZY. No. No, don't work for them. I was associated with them, for a while.

DICK. A volunteer?

LIZZY. No. A beneficiary.

DICK. Oh.

LIZZY. They helped me through a difficult time.

DICK. Oh.

LIZZY. After my dad left, and my mum couldn't cope. Years ago.

DICK. Ah. In Peckham.

LIZZY. Yes.

DICK. Which is how you met –

LIZZY. Sally. Yes. And Christopher.

DICK. Terrible business.

LIZZY. Yes.

DICK. Bloody brave of you to come for Christmas, so soon after.

LIZZY *shrugs.*

LIZZY. Nice of them to ask me.

DICK. You must miss him terribly.

LIZZY. Mm.

Pause. LIZZY wants to end the conversation. DICK doesn't.

DICK. Did you know the boys who killed him?

*LIZZY looks at DICK, horrified. DICK realises what he's
just said.*

No. No, of course not. Absolutely not. Why would you have?
Of course. Goodness. Sorry.

LIZZY. Don't worry.

DICK. I mean. It must be awful for them. Obviously it's awful
for Richard and Sally – we can't even imagine. But those
boys – such deprivation. To just go for someone like – that –
just *go* at a stranger – (*Sort of gently mimes 'stabbing'*.) he
was breaking up a fight, wasn't he? That's what Sally told us.

LIZZY. Is it?

DICK. Mm. So they had an incentive to kill. Their blood was
up. But the *violence* of the thing – it's like a Lynda LaPlante.
They'd have to be *wounded*, *broken* people to do a thing like
that. What is it? *Disenfranchised*. Yes. I've got all sorts of
theories about the whole business, if you'd – I mean, now's
probably not the time.

A tight smile from LIZZY.

LIZZY. No, probably not.

DICK. But maybe if you came on the Boxing Day walk? That's
always good for a chinwag.

LIZZY. Yes – that might be… fun.

DICK's not listening.

DICK. Mmm. It's very rum. Have you read *Oliver Twist*? It's
ever so good on all this kind of stuff. The seedy underbelly
of humanity. Urban rot.

LIZZY. No, I haven't.

RICHARD *comes in – fresh from the shed.*

RICHARD. Ho ho ho, is everyone feeling festive?

LIZZY. Certainly are.

DICK. Lizzy and I were having a chat about social deprivation.

RICHARD. I'm very sorry to have missed that.

RICHARD *goes over and picks up a bottle of gin.*

DICK. Thought you were on the Scotch.

RICHARD. I'm freestyling. Where's dinner?

LIZZY. Sally says five minutes.

RICHARD. Ugh. A man could die of hunger here. (*Calls into the kitchen.*) Sally?

DAISY *comes in from the kitchen, holding a bowl filled with cranberries and glitter and topped with holly.*

What the hell is that?

DAISY. It's my festive centrepiece.

DAISY *dumps the centrepiece on the table and turns to* DICK.

I just spoke to Lynda, Dick, my primary contact at the centre. And she says that I need to face my fears and honestly tell you where I've been, in order to prevent further misunderstandings and conversational awkwardnesses. Also, I need to own my own power.

RICHARD. She's so laid-back, isn't she? Easy-going. A real charmer.

DAISY. So I'm going to tell you. I've been in a private psychiatric clinic.

DICK. Oh.

DAISY. Did you hear that, Dick? A private psychiatric clinic.

DICK. Yes.

RICHARD. She wasn't mad enough for the NHS.

DAISY. I've been receiving treatment following a period of mental-health disturbance. Which is not a cause for guilt or shame. Rather, a cause for celebration.

RICHARD. She's had a nervous breakthrough.

DAISY (*to* RICHARD). Stop making jokes! Stop it! It's not funny! I'm not funny! I am not a cause for humour!

RICHARD. Too bloody right you're not. Twenty grand up the spout and –

DAISY *turns to face the wall.*

DAISY. One-two-three-CALM-two-three-one-two-three-CALM-two-three –

RICHARD. Oh, God. Sally, she's doing it again!

SALLY *comes in holding the big sauté pan of chopped-up sprouts. She's followed by* VALERIE, *carrying the rest of the dinner.*

DAISY. One-two-three-CALM-two-three-one-two-three-CALM-two-three –

SALLY. What? Oh. No, it's fine. She told me about that. It's a good thing. We should encourage her.

DAISY. One-two-three-CALM-two-three – DONE!

DAISY *swings round with a smile.*

Is it time for dinner?

SALLY. It certainly is.

DAISY. Brilliant. I'm hungry.

Everyone stares at DAISY, *confused. The kitten mewls from the cage.*

Scene Three

Later. They've just settled down to the Christmas Eve meal. It's going well. Conversation bouncing along. Already an empty wine bottle on the sideboard, and half-full one in the middle of the table.

DAISY's sitting at the head of the table – placed so she seems a bit apart from the main group. At the other end of the table – facing her – the empty place. Holly in the wine glass.

SALLY. Christopher believed in Father Christmas until he was fifteen.

VALERIE (*laughing*). He didn't!

SALLY. He did! Well, he did and he didn't. We always used to say – 'Father Christmas is real, but when you stop believing in him he stops coming. And that's when Mum and Dad take over.'

DICK. That's actually very clever.

VALERIE. When did you stop believing in Father Christmas, Daisy?

DAISY. I never believed in him.

RICHARD. You bloody did! It was always you and Christopher, up on Christmas morning. Five a.m. Tramping all over me to open your chocolate coins.

DAISY. Well, maybe when I was very tiny.

VALERIE. You used to love Christmas. I remember us coming round with Jennifer – you must have been about ten – and you'd been given a thing. A mechanical thing, with penguins, where you slot it all together and the penguins go up the hill and then race down again. It was ever such fun – what was it called?

SALLY. The Penguin Race.

VALERIE. Yes! And every time the penguins raced down the slide, you'd try to run once round the coffee table. You wanted to see if you could beat them. I don't think you ever did.

DAISY. No, I never did.

VALERIE. You were such a funny little girl. All rosy cheeks and smiles and running around – what was that nickname, what did we used to call you?

DICK. Crazy Daisy!

DAISY *stops eating suddenly, puts her knife and fork down and stares at her plate. Very awkward pause.* SALLY *clears her throat.*

SALLY. I wonder what Jennifer'll be doing for Christmas dinner. Throwing a shrimp on the barbie, no doubt.

DICK. Ha! No shrimp. Not in her condition.

LIZZY. Is she pregnant?

DICK. Mm. Turkey-baster baby.

SALLY. I had no idea! That's wonder/ful.

RICHARD. It's Christmassy, at least.

SALLY. Who's the father?

DICK. They got the sperm from the internet.

RICHARD. Dreadful word, 'sperm'.

VALERIE. It's a very well-thought-of sperm bank. Rocket scientists. Lumberjacks. Concert pianists. I mean, obviously it's not what we'd imagined / but –

RICHARD. 'Sperm.' Ugh. '*Sperm.*'

LIZZY. You're going to be grandparents. That's wicked. Congratulations.

VALERIE. Thank you, Lizzy.

DICK. Well, we don't actually know that for certain. They mixed both their eggs up with the sp– the stuff, and just sort of shoved it all in Jennifer. So it could belong to either of them. In another time and place that'd be thought of as a predicament. Now, apparently, it's a cause for celebration.

VALERIE. Dick! We're delighted. He's just being a curmudgeon. He's very liberal really.

DICK. Well, yes, I am, in theory. People can do whatever they want with themselves in *theory*, that's their business. But I'd always imagined dandling my grandchild on my knee, you know? My grandchild. Not some sort of composite lesbian turkey-baster lumberjack sperm-thing.

LIZZY. I'm sure you'll love it when you meet it. All that'll melt away. You'll just be... you know, Granddad.

SALLY. That's a lovely thing to say, Lizzy.

LIZZY *smiles at* SALLY.

DAISY. Yes, Lizzy's lovely, isn't she? Aren't we all lucky to have Lizzy here? Hooray for Lizzy. Well done, Lizzy. Brilliant.

DAISY *jams her fork hard into a potato.*

Awkward pause. Everyone eats.

RICHARD. Apparently sperm-bank babies are five times more likely to turn into criminals.

SALLY. That's not true.

RICHARD. It is. I read a thing in the *Mail* –

SALLY. We don't read the *Mail*.

RICHARD. I do. Did you know that our son being murdered will have adversely affected the price of our house? Bet you didn't know that.

DAISY. Dad's got more right-wing since Christopher died. It makes him feel safe.

Everyone ignores DAISY.

SALLY. He doesn't read the *Mail*.

RICHARD. I read it online when you're out. I read the *Daily Mail* online, and I wear those tartan trousers you hate, and I eat Burger King.

SALLY. He doesn't. He's lying. We haven't got a Burger King.

DICK. They're building a Kentucky Fried Chicken on the Maldeston roundabout.

SALLY. They're never.

VALERIE. They are! Next to the BP garage. We saw a planning-permission-sign thingy when we stopped for petrol.

DICK *turns to* LIZZY.

DICK. Bet there's lots of Kentucky Fried Chicken where you come from, eh, Lizzy? 'Peckham.' The smoke.

LIZZY. I don't really eat it.

DICK. McDonald's? Pizza Hut? Chicken Cottage?

LIZZY *laughs*.

LIZZY. Well, yes, all right. But only if I'm really desperate.

DICK. Mm. Want to keep an eye on that lovely figure of yours.

VALERIE. Dick!

DICK. What? She's an attractive girl. Don't see too many of her type round these parts.

LIZZY *looks embarrassed*.

SALLY. Lizzy's a wonderful cook. She cooked a lovely meal for me and Daisy and Christoph/er –

RICHARD. Could you pass the cabbage?

SALLY. Sprouts.

VALERIE *passes* RICHARD *the sprouts*.

No, we all went round to her flat –

DICK. In Peckham?

DAISY. Yes.

DICK. How did you get there?

VALERIE. I imagine they went on the bus, Dick.

DAISY. They didn't need an armoured car.

DICK. Oh. Ha ha! Very funny.

SALLY. We all went round to Lizzy's, and what did you cook us? What was that?

LIZZY. Jerk chicken.

SALLY. Well, it was wonderful. It was a real treat.

LIZZY. It was from a packet.

SALLY. Even so. Then we went to see that film – with all the ski/ing.

DAISY. *Chalet Girl*.

SALLY. It was ever so funny.

DAISY. It was shit.

SALLY. Daisy!

DAISY. Well, it was.

LIZZY. I enjoyed it.

DAISY (*hostile*). Did you?

Pause.

SALLY. Lizzy and Christopher had some wonderful times together.

LIZZY. We did. We really did. We had lots of fun.

SALLY. I remember when you both ran that five K. For City Mates. Poor Chrissy wasn't quite as fit as he thought he was, was he?

LIZZY. No. (*Laughs.*) He did his best, though.

SALLY. What was it? Fifty-five minutes?

LIZZY. They didn't write the time on his certificate. They just put...

SALLY/LIZZY. 'Slightly slower than your granny!'

SALLY, LIZZY *and* VALERIE *laugh.*

DAISY. That was because he smoked. He smoked forty cigarettes a day. It's hard to run fast when you smoke forty cigarettes a day

SALLY. Now, Daisy, you're exaggerating, he only ever had the odd one or two. Did you ever see him smoke, Lizzy?

LIZZY. No, can't say I ever / did.

DAISY. Can't say you ever saw him do anything bad, can you? No one did. Saint Christopher. Never put a foot wrong. Perfect Christopher. Right?

LIZZY *meets* DAISY*'s eye for a moment. Looks away.*

SALLY. No one's accusing anyone of being perfect, Daisy. We're just reminiscing. We're honouring the happy times that Lizzy and Christopher spent together. Is that a problem?

DAISY. No. No, not for me. If Lizzy can stomach it, then that's fine. Fine. By. Me.

DAISY *has served herself an enormous amount of sprouts, and is trying to mould them into a small structure on her plate.*

SALLY *eyes her nervously.*

SALLY. Daisy, what are you doing?

DAISY. I'm building a sprout house.

DICK. What's that?

DAISY. A house of sprouts. I used to do it when I was little, remember, Mum? When we used to have whole sprouts. They're easier to build with than these.

SALLY. They're Jamie Oliver. Stop that, Daisy, it's odd.

DAISY. Well, we're reminiscing, aren't we? So I thought we could reminisce about the sprout house.

SALLY (*very slowly and deliberately*). Now, Daisy, if you want to discuss the sprout house then I'm sure that we can –

DAISY. Don't talk to me like I'm a mental patient. I'm just trying to build a fucking sprout house.

DAISY gets up and walks over to the kitchen door.

SALLY. Daisy, where are you going?

DAISY. To get some liquorice.

SALLY. Why?

DAISY. *For the chimney!*

DAISY goes into the kitchen. Leaves the door open.

RICHARD. Should we call Lynda? Is this a cuckoo's-nest situation?

SALLY. Oh, she's fine. She's always been highly strung. Just ignore her.

DAISY shouts back from the kitchen.

DAISY (*offstage*). *Don't you fucking dare ignore me! Don't you dare!*

A few pots and pans bang about in the kitchen.

A particularly loud bang, and the sound of something breaking. SALLY *winces.*

VALERIE. Well, something's clearly upset her.

LIZZY. I think I've upset her.

SALLY. Now, what could you possibly have done to upset her? No, it's her. She's in mental disarray. Just leave her to it.

Everyone eats. A bit awkward.

VALERIE. Where are your family this Christmas, Lizzy?

LIZZY. I'm not really sure. We're not close.

VALERIE. That's a shame.

LIZZY. I don't mind. Christmas isn't a big thing for me. I worked until last night. So it's just a day, really.

DICK. Lizzy's a fashion PR.

VALERIE. Are you? Well done, you!

LIZZY. Thanks.

SALLY. Lizzy was featured in a magazine, weren't you, Lizzy? A woman's glossy.

DICK*'s interested.*

DICK. Oh, were you now?

LIZZY *looks a bit embarrassed.*

LIZZY. Yeah. It was fun. It was just a silly / thing.

SALLY. Well, I wouldn't call it silly, not in the slightest. What were you – ?

LIZZY. *Estelle* magazine. November's 'Interesting Inspirational Female'.

DICK. Why were you in the magazine?

LIZZY. Well, they thought it was interesting, I suppose. That I do the job I do. Having come from the background I'm from.

DICK. Inspirational.

LIZZY *smiles politely.*

DAISY *steams back in from the kitchen, holding a pillowcase full of stuff.*

DAISY. Yes. Apparently it's really impressive that Lizzy's a fashion PR, because she grew up on a council estate with an alcoholic mum, and didn't go to university. Whereas if *I* decided to be a fashion PR, then it would be all 'Oh, la la la, vapid little posh girl does vapid little dumb job, oh *quelle surprise*, how predictable, how we all hate her what a massive dick she is.' Ha ha.

SALLY. Daisy! Stop it!

DAISY *holds up the pillowcase.*

DAISY. I found this sack full of shit make-up from Superdrug. I dropped a glass of wine in it but I thought I could use the eyeliners to make windows for the sprout house.

SALLY. Oh, Daisy! That was supposed to be Lizzy's stocking! Lizzy, I'm so sorry. Daisy, you're appalling.

LIZZY. It's fine, honestly. You didn't need to get me anything.

DAISY. You're so humble, aren't you, Lizzy? So gracious. Regal. No wonder everyone thinks you're just so totally lovely. So totally fucking cheese-grater-across-the-knuckles, slit-your-wrists marvellous to be around.

LIZZY *stares at the table.* SALLY *talks to* VALERIE *and* DICK.

SALLY. Lizzy and Daisy can talk to one another like this, you see. They've known each other for years. They're like sisters.

DAISY. No, we're not.

DAISY *sits down at the table. Aggressively eats the sprout house. Everyone eats.* RICHARD *finishes his drink and pours himself another. It's very awkward.*

VALERIE (*to* LIZZY). So, Lizzy, you must have known the Lllewellyns for a long time now?

LIZZY. Yeah – I mean, God. Twelve, thirteen years. I've been here loads.

DAISY. As part of Mum's social-inclusion drive.

LIZZY *and* VALERIE *ignore her.* VALERIE *continues to listen intently to* DAISY.

LIZZY. I used to come down for summers. To see the countryside and stuff. I'd literally never seen a cow before I came here. I was like 'Oh my God, it's eating the ground.'

VALERIE *laughs.*

SALLY. I was Lizzy's mentor. I volunteered for City Mates –

RICHARD. Mid-life crisis.

SALLY. – and I really couldn't have been luckier, could I? Lovely Lizzy.

LIZZY smiles awkwardly.

VALERIE. And Christopher had decided to volunteer as well –

SALLY. Mm. For his gap year.

VALERIE. What a good boy he was.

SALLY. Mm.

They all eat in silence. Bit awkward.

DICK. Brave boy.

DAISY. Why brave?

DICK. Well, you know… getting right in the thick of it. The gangs. Estates. Doing good works. Quite like, you know – Jesus.

LIZZY smiles and nods.

DAISY snorts.

RICHARD. Something wrong, Daisy?

DAISY. No, nothing. Just… Jesus.

DICK. Well, it's terrifying, isn't it? What goes on.

DAISY. I don't know, Dick. What goes on?

DICK. Well – all the bloodshed. Youth at war. The news. It's not the sort of thing you expect someone you know to get caught up in, is all. Least of all an *innocent boy* –

VALERIE. Sally, are you comfortable talking about this?

RICHARD. I'm not. Drink, anyone? More drink?

Everyone ignores RICHARD.

SALLY. Yes. We're very open. This is fascinating. I'm enjoying it.

DICK *turns to* LIZZY.

DICK. I mean, obviously *you've* somehow managed to rise above it. And I doff my cap to you –

LIZZY. Thank you.

DICK. – you're clearly the – the beautiful rose atop the dung-heap –

DAISY. Dung-heap? Oh, Dick. Valerie's right. You are a true liberal.

LIZZY. It's fine. Really. It's just a turn of phrase.

DAISY. Isn't he annoying you, Lizzy?

LIZZY *stares at her plate*.

No, really. Doesn't it piss you off? Middle-class wankers –

DICK. Hey!

SALLY. Daisy!

DAISY. – like Dick referring to the social class which you were born and brought up in as a 'dung-heap'. Because I'd imagine that that would really bother you.

SALLY. Lizzy knows how to take a compliment, Daisy, that's all. She's being pleasant. She's honouring Christmas. I think we should all honour Christmas.

DAISY. Yes, Christmas. Good old Christmas. Let's all chop ourselves up into bits and sacrifice ourselves at the altar of *Christmas*.

RICHARD. You know, right now that doesn't seem such a bad idea.

DICK. No, I didn't mean – look, I think you're all marvellous, is all I'm saying.

DAISY. Who's marvellous?

DICK. The lot of you. Christopher, for giving his life in the service of others. All the… troubled people for just… being troubled. And Sally and Richard, for continuing to support the work of this City Mates thing when their son died from it.

DAISY. 'Died from it'?

SALLY. How's everyone for sprouts?

DAISY. Fine, thank you. (*Turns back to* DICK.) He wasn't murdered by City Mates, you know. City Mates is a small charity providing support and connections for vulnerable young people in two inner-city boroughs. It's a benevolent set-up. It's not the mob. Unless it is. Is it, Lizzy? Was Christopher the *innocent* victim of *nefarious* forces, conspiring to kill?

LIZZY. No. No, he wasn't.

Bit of a pause. DICK *pipes up.*

DICK. No – but he was murdered by – well, people who might turn out to be the sort of people who –

VALERIE. Dick, I think we've talked about this quite enough.

DAISY. What sort of people, Dick? Poor people?

DICK. No! People from – people who've – not necessarily enjoyed the advantages that people like Valerie and I –

DAISY. Black people, then?

DICK. No, absolutely not! I never said that – I would *never* say that, *never* –

VALERIE. Daisy, I'm sure he didn't mean / that.

DAISY. Got lots of black friends, have you, Dick?

DICK *thumps the table.*

DICK. Not relevant! Not relevant!

DAISY. Or do you read *National Geographic*? Plenty of them there. Bet you'd love to see Lizzy with her tits out, full tribal costume, banging a drum.

SALLY. Daisy, you stop this *right now* –

LIZZY. Daisy, shut up.

DAISY. Don't you fucking tell me what to do.

DICK. No – God – absolutely not – it's – I simply – we've got our wires crossed. This is just – it's just – oh, there's a phrase for this – it's –

DAISY. The subtle racism of being a patronising cunt.

Pause. Everyone's shocked.

DICK. How *dare* you! *How dare you?* I have *never* in my *life* been called –

VALERIE *grabs* DICK*'s arm.*

VALERIE. Dick, leave it. Please. Leave it.

SALLY. Just ignore Daisy, everyone. She doesn't mean it. She's not herself. She's not well in the head.

DAISY. Isn't she?

SALLY. Can we just enjoy our dinner? Please, can we all enjoy our dinner?

They all eat. Long pause. The kitten mewls from the cage.

RICHARD (*a bit nasty*). *Lovely* sprouts, Sally. *Lovely.*

SALLY *doesn't respond. Another long pause.*

VALERIE. Dick isn't a racist, you know.

DAISY. Just a homophobe.

SALLY *slams her cutlery on the table.*

SALLY. *Daisy!*

DICK. I didn't come here to be spoken to like this.

RICHARD *fills* DICK*'s glass, and his own.*

RICHARD. Just booze through it, Dick. Only way.

Pause. The kitten mewls from his cage. They all eat.
VALERIE clears her throat.

VALERIE. Do you still volunteer, Lizzy? For City Mates?

LIZZY. No. I did for a few years. Then it got a bit… well, the mood changed.

VALERIE. How so?

LIZZY. It just evolved, I suppose.

DAISY *snorts again*.

DAISY. That's not what you wrote on your blog. 'Evolved.'

VALERIE. Oh, do you keep a blog, Lizzy? Jennifer's been keeping a baby blog –

LIZZY. Kept. Kept a blog. I took it down. It was rubbish.

DAISY. I found it fascinating. Really fascinating. Especially the comment you wrote about City Mates.

LIZZY. Daisy, please don't –

DAISY. What was it – it was – oh yes. 'Overrun with middle-class gap-year wankers trying to be good.' Isn't that what you wrote, Lizzy?

LIZZY. I was –

DAISY. Didn't you write that, Lizzy?

LIZZY. I didn't mean / it.

DAISY. But you did write it.

LIZZY. Yeah. Yeah I did. But I didn't mean it.

DAISY. Why might you have written it, then? Hmm?

LIZZY. I don't know.

Long, long pause. The kitten mewls from inside the cage.

DAISY. Did you think that Christopher was a wanker, Lizzy?

SALLY. *Daisy!* Go to your room.

DAISY. No. I won't. You can't make me. Did you think he was a wanker, Lizzy?

LIZZY. No, of course not.

SALLY. Lizzy loved Christopher.

DAISY. Oh. So he was more like Jesus, then. Like Dick said. Jesus.

LIZZY. Well –

DAISY. Or not like Jesus?

LIZZY *stares at her plate.*

Simple question. Wanker, or Jesus? I suppose if you thought he was a wanker, then you wouldn't have come, would you? So he must have been like Jesus.

LIZZY (*quietly, near the end of her tether*). I came because I was invited.

DAISY. You should have said no.

LIZZY. I wish I had. I really really wish I had.

DAISY. Are you going to be honest, Lizzy? Or are you just going to keep playing along with all the bullshit? I thought you were better than this. Not much better, but better.

DICK. What's going on?

RICHARD. Fuck knows.

SALLY. Right! That's it. I'm calling Lynda.

DAISY. Oh, great. Pack me off back to the clinic. Tie my hands behind my back and heave me into the big white van. All for trying to inject a little bit of truth into the situation.

SALLY. 'Truth'? You're just being offensive, Daisy. I fail to see where truth comes into this.

DAISY. It doesn't, apparently. *Apparently,* what happened is that Lizzy and Christopher had one of the most beautiful, healthy relationships known to man jogging wild and free round Battersea Park, arm in arm, neither of them so much as smoking a fag, before they lovingly separated, immediately after which Christopher, en route to his world-saving charity-helping super-interview, nobly stepped in to prevent a fight between two gangs of undesirables – that's the dung-heap to you, Dick –

DICK. Hey!

DAISY. – during the course of which he was killed. Boom, hero.

SALLY (*irritable*). That is what happened. That's the truth.

DAISY. Is it? Is it, Lizzy?

LIZZY *gets up*.

LIZZY. Look, you guys have clearly got some issues here –

RICHARD. I'll say we do.

LIZZY. I shouldn't have come –

LIZZY *gets up and goes over to the door.*

DAISY. Where do you think you're / going?

SALLY *addresses* VALERIE, RICHARD *and* DICK.

SALLY. She's mad. Daisy's gone completely mad. No one listen to a word she says.

LIZZY. Home.

DAISY. And how are you going to do that? Christmas Eve, nine p.m. No trains tonight, and all the taxi drivers are pissed. You're more than welcome to walk, but I wouldn't imagine those princess shoes would do you any favours.

LIZZY *sits down in an armchair. Puts her head in her hands. Groans.*

LIZZY. Oh, God…

DAISY. Lovely. Well, now you're sitting down, you can tell everybody the truth about Christopher.

SALLY. He was a hero. My boy was a hero.

VALERIE. Daisy? Lizzy? What's going on?

SALLY. Daisy – you said – you promised we could have Christmas nicely, you promised you'd be good –

DAISY*'s still glaring at* LIZZY.

DAISY. That was before she turned up. The hero thing – fine. The Foundation, I can handle. The poem. The candle. A year's worth of bollocks. Fine. Whatever you need. But *her* – joining in? Pretending – when she was *so close*, when she *knew* – it's too much.

RICHARD. Knew what?

Everyone looks at LIZZY. *The kitten mewls from his cage.*

LIZZY. I don't know what to say.

SALLY. Then don't say anything. Just don't say anything.

RICHARD. No, I think she should say something. Whatever it is Daisy wants her to say, I think she should say it. Might give us all a chance of leaving this fucking table before midnight.

LIZZY*'s in agony.* RICHARD *turns to her.*

Well? Lizzy? Best spit it out, whatever it is.

DAISY. Yes, Lizzy. Spit it out.

LIZZY. No. This isn't fair.

RICHARD. Life's not fair. Now – knew what?

LIZZY (*quietly*). Seriously, fuck this.

RICHARD. Yes! I quite agree! Fuck this! Fuck the lot of it, fuck it hard, all the way to next Christmas! But first – *knew what*?

Long pause. LIZZY *stares at the floor. She really doesn't want to say what she's about to say.*

LIZZY. Okay. You know that him and me were together. And then we broke up.

SALLY. Because he went to Thailand. And you didn't want to be long-distance.

LIZZY. We broke up because of the way he was living his life.

SALLY. I don't understand.

LIZZY. Generally being a… not being very nice. You know. Drinking. Drugs. Messing around.

SALLY. He was young.

LIZZY *stares at the floor.*

Lizzy? He was on his gap year. Everyone's a bit silly on their gap year. Everyone –

LIZZY. Everyone kicks off the day with a couple of lines? Everyone's off for three days at a time, fuck knows where, comes back bleeding? Everyone buys drugs from estate kids, carts them back to Aldeburgh, sells them on for double what they paid? Everyone plays the big man, thinks they're it when *they don't fucking understand what they're mixed up / with* –

VALERIE. Lizzy, stop it!

LIZZY *stops, shocked at herself.*

RICHARD. No, don't stop, Lizzy. I think we're finally getting somewhere. So, yes. Drugs. Estates. Aldeburgh. Bleeding. Gangs. Fascinating! Anything else?

LIZZY. That's it. He took drugs. He'd started dealing. And that was why he was where he was when he –

SALLY. He was on his way to an interview. He was going to be a mentor.

LIZZY *shakes her head, stares at the floor. Silence.*

He broke up a fight. Lizzy? He saw a fight, and he intervened to try and stop it, and he got hurt.

LIZZY*'s still looking at the floor.*

LIZZY. That's not what happened. It was – he was in over his head. He owed money. He mouthed off. End of.

DAISY. So – not like Jesus.

LIZZY *doesn't respond.*

SALLY. You're lying, Lizzy. Daisy made you lie.

DAISY. Oh, for fuck's sake –

SALLY*'s gone glassy. Dazed.*

SALLY. Daisy, why would you make her say these things?
Why?

DAISY. Because it's the truth. Isn't it, Lizzy?

LIZZY *nods.* DAISY *turns back to* SALLY.

And you need to face up to it! You need to know – if those
boys go to trial in the new year, this is all going to come out.
You think they've not told their lawyers every little thing
about your lovely son? All his little ways? And you think the
press won't leap on it? They lap this shit up. Your precious
Daily Mail –

SALLY. We don't read the *Mail*.

RICHARD. I do.

DAISY. Your precious *Daily Mail*'s going to be all over it like a
leopard on a corpse. 'Fifty-Thousand-Pound-a-Year Public
School Couldn't Save Him From Himself' – 'Smoking Joints
in Their Million-Pound Family Home.' Pictures of our
holidays, years back – they'll find a way to get hold of them.
Whack them up on the website next to a picture of Kim
Kardashian's armpits. Slip Valerie and Dick a few hundred
quid / for a quote.

DICK. Hey!

DAISY. They're going to rip the rotting carcass of our family
life apart, and they're going to shit all over it. And, Mum –
nice hair. Just had that done, did you? They'll love that.
Symptom of your total fucking wrongness. 'Off at the salon
as her junkie son lay dead.' 'Middle-class malaise.' 'Tip of
the iceberg.' Big think-piece. Editorial. We're all on trial, the
lot of us. And your little fairy-princess-castle-Jesus-hero
story might be fooling everyone now, but come January, it's

over. And you need to fucking face up to that. (*Running out of steam*.) You have to face up to things. They – they say in the clinic… you have to – face it all. Or you get more hurt.

Silence. SALLY*'s whey-faced, very still*.

VALERIE. But that can't be true. I mean, if Sally had known then she wouldn't have spent the last year –

SALLY (*quietly, looking at her plate*). I knew.

VALERIE. What?

SALLY. I knew. I'm his mother. I could see inside him. Since he was born, before he was born. I knew him, every twitch. He was going, long before he went. I knew that. (*Pause*.) I just wanted to give him one last Christmas.

Everyone's quiet. A long pause.

DICK (*with some satisfaction*). Seven.

VALERIE (*quietly, irritated*). What?

DICK. I've got seven black friends. Or I have had, over the course of my life. And four gay friends, not including my daughter. And I'm on nodding terms with three bisexuals, which must surely be above the national average. So.

VALERIE (*quietly*). Dick.

LIZZY*'s looking at* SALLY*, concerned*.

LIZZY. I'm sorry, Sally. I'm really sorry.

DAISY. What are you sorry about? Everyone knows the truth now. It's better. Isn't it, Mum? It's better? Right? Mum?

SALLY *suddenly springs into life*.

SALLY. Is it? *Is it better?* Well, if Daisy says it's better then it must be better, mustn't it? Because Daisy's had all of her wonderful expensive therapy, so Daisy knows best! It's better that everything's broken, isn't it, Daisy? Shall we break some more things? Would they like that, the people at the clinic? Some lovely healthy smashing? Yes. I think they would.

SALLY *throws her plate at* DAISY. DAISY *screams and ducks, the plate smashes against the wall.*

Isn't that right? Don't you know best, Daisy?

DAISY *looks terrified.*

DAISY. Mum – I –

SALLY. What's that? Speak up! Everybody needs to speak up and tell the truth, don't they? Don't they, Daisy?

SALLY *throws another plate.*

'The truth will set us free!' Right, Daisy?

SALLY*'s about to throw another plate* – VALERIE *jumps up and restrains her.* DAISY *falls back into the Christmas tree; it topples over sideways.*

SALLY *sits back down in her chair crying.* VALERIE *holds her.*

DAISY. I'm sorry, Mum. I'm really sorry.

RICHARD *sits back in his chair and lights a cigarette.*

RICHARD. I told you we should have gone to the Caribbean.

The kitten mewls from his cage.

End of Act One.

ACT TWO

Scene One

Living room.

Middle of the night.

It's been tidied a little bit since the previous scene – plates piled on the sideboard, etc. – but it's still far from pristine. The Christmas tree is back up, but propped up against the wall.

The room is lit only by the fairy lights on the tree.

The kitten mewls from his cage.

DAISY *walks in, wearing pyjamas, a dressing gown and big furry slippers. She goes over to the kitten cage, and opens it.*

DAISY. It's okay, little one. We're going to be friends.

> DAISY *carefully lifts the kitten out of the cage. He's tiny and biscuit coloured.*

> Shh shh. We're going to have a lovely Christmas, you and me.

> DAISY *takes Mr Biscuits over to an armchair. Sits down. She kisses him on the top of the head.*

> Did you know that on Christmas Eve at midnight, all the animals speak? You probably didn't know that, did you? Because you're ever so new. A brand-new thing.

> *The kitten mewls.*

> It's a good world, Mr Biscuits. There's lots to eat and drink, and soft places everywhere. And I'm going to love you very much.

> DAISY *stares intently at the kitten.*

> Say something, Mr Biscuits. It's your Christmas responsibility to say some words.

*There's a disturbance behind the fireplace. Kicking,
swearing. A pair of old black, hobnail boots and the bottom
of some red trousers – trimmed with white fur – appear in
the fireplace. It seems that Father Christmas is coming down
the chimney.*

DAISY*'s scared.*

Hello? Father Christmas? *Hello?*

FATHER CHRISTMAS *speaks in an affected and deep jolly
voice. It's clearly someone dressed up as Father Christmas,
not the real Father Christmas.*

FATHER CHRISTMAS (*still half up the chimney*). Yo ho ho!
Have you got a mince pie for me, little girl?

DAISY (*afraid*). No, I'm sorry. I didn't know you were coming.

FATHER CHRISTMAS *lands in the fireplace. Scrambles out
into the living room. Dusts himself off.*

FATHER CHRISTMAS. Yo ho ho!

DAISY. There's some mince pies in the kitchen, if you want
them –

FATHER CHRISTMAS *takes off his beard, hat and jacket.
It's* CHRISTOPHER, *nineteen,* DAISY*'s dead brother.*

*He's wearing a white T-shirt, covered in fresh-looking
bloodstains. Still in the Father Christmas trousers and boots.*

Christopher!

CHRISTOPHER *smiles. He seems calm. Detached.*

CHRISTOPHER. Happy Christmas.

CHRISTOPHER *wanders over to* DAISY. DAISY*'s
mesmerised by the sight of him.* CHRISTOPHER *takes in the
room. He's not seen it for a while.*

There's no star on the tree.

DAISY. No one here to put it on.

CHRISTOPHER. Dad's tall enough.

DAISY *shakes her head.*

DAISY. Your job.

CHRISTOPHER *sees* SALLY*'s strung-up oranges Christmas decoration.*

CHRISTOPHER. Are those oranges?

DAISY. It's a new decoration. Mum wanted to ring the changes.

CHRISTOPHER *sees Mr Biscuits.* DAISY*'s holding tight to him.*

CHRISTOPHER. What's that?

DAISY. He's called Mr Biscuits.

CHRISTOPHER. Where's Buttons?

DAISY. Buttons died. Just after you did.

CHRISTOPHER *wanders over to the mantelpiece. Sees the photographs of him, Buttons and the old lady.*

CHRISTOPHER. Oh. Right.

DAISY. We didn't save you any dinner. Have you had dinner?

CHRISTOPHER *sits in an armchair. Curls up a bit – comfortable. At home. Smiles at* DAISY.

CHRISTOPHER. You don't have to be nice to me.

DAISY. Do they feed you? Where you are? Do you need food? (*Pause.*) After you – after it – afterwards – that was all I could think. What a waste of all that food you ate, all through your whole life. You don't need any of it any more. (*Pause.*) Are you okay, Christopher? Are you okay now?

CHRISTOPHER. That's up to you.

CHRISTOPHER *gets up again. Looks around the room.*

Heard you nailed it at the funeral.

DAISY. You weren't there?

CHRISTOPHER *shakes his head.*

CHRISTOPHER. Not my scene.

DAISY. Well, I said – it was quite hard. But I just said some
words about you. Like, a sort of a free-association thing.
Happy words, like 'cricket'. 'Fajitas.' 'Zorro.' 'Blond.'
'Snowboard.' 'Gentle.' 'Funny.' 'Weird.' 'Loving.' 'Peaceful.'
'Fun.' Then some less happy words. Like 'lonely'. 'Space.'
'Edgy.' 'Oddity.' 'Oblivion.' 'Wild.' 'Crash.' And then I sort
of pre-empted people by saying that I know you're not
supposed to say the bad words at a funeral because you're
meant to be all sycophantic and stuff when someone's died,
but that you were all the good words and all the bad words
mixed up, and you were still perfect. Just the way you were.

CHRISTOPHER *likes this. Nods. He's not really listening.
Too busy looking round the room.*

CHRISTOPHER. 'Perfect.' Love it.

DAISY. And then I said 'fuck' a few times then I said sorry for
saying fuck in church. And then I said 'no actually I'm not
fucking sorry,' and then I suddenly thought of loads more
things I wanted to say, but Uncle Pete came up to the pulpit
and got me and took me outside and tried to make me feel
better by giving me a Strepsil. Which was a bit weird.

CHRISTOPHER *nods.*

CHRISTOPHER. Sweet.

DAISY *giggles.*

What?

DAISY (*mimicking him*). 'Suh-weet.' You're *still* doing the
mockney thing. Like, post-mortem. Give it up, mate.

CHRISTOPHER *chuckles.* CHRISTOPHER *and* DAISY
stand and look at each other for a moment. DAISY*'s
completely thrilled to see him again.*

Mum planted snowdrops in the garden for you. A whole bed
of them.

CHRISTOPHER. Snowdrops? Really? Huh.

CHRISTOPHER*'s amused by this. Continues looking round the room.*

Where's the Penguin Race? It should be here.

DAISY. It doesn't work.

CHRISTOPHER. Oh.

DAISY. Nothing works any more. You need to come back and make everything work again.

CHRISTOPHER. Daisy –

DAISY. Just be here tomorrow! Please. One day. You can do that. Wherever you are, whoever's in charge of it – we can negotiate. One more day.

CHRISTOPHER. You know that can't happen.

DAISY. Please.

DAISY*'s near to tears.*

CHRISTOPHER *shakes his head.*

Pause. CHRISTOPHER *and* DAISY *look at each other.*

CHRISTOPHER. We can dance.

CHRISTOPHER *clicks his fingers and a Christmas carol comes on, 'Silent Night'.*

DAISY. We can't dance to this.

CHRISTOPHER. Chicken. You've not even tried.

CHRISTOPHER *holds once hand out, palm facing* DAISY. DAISY *places her palm against his, still holding Mr Biscuits in the other hand.* CHRISTOPHER *circles his palm slowly outwards.* DAISY *does the same, mirroring him. She's staring intently into his eyes.* CHRISTOPHER *looks pretty relaxed.*

DAISY *giggles.*

DAISY. This isn't dancing. You liar.

CHRISTOPHER *closes his hand around* DAISY*'s, and gives it a squeeze.*

CHRISTOPHER. Bye, Daisy.

CHRISTOPHER *lets go of* DAISY*'s hand.*

DAISY *(panicked).* Don't go! Please! Don't go! Is it because I called you a liar?

CHRISTOPHER. Got to go! Bye!

CHRISTOPHER *runs out.* DAISY *watches him go.*

DAISY. Christopher? Please? *Christopher! Come back!*

He's gone. DAISY *wipes away a tear, and kisses Mr Biscuits on top of his head.*

She stands alone in the living room. 'Silent Night' fades away.

Scene Two

Living room.

Christmas morning. The living room as it was in the previous scene. Half-cleared-up.

Mewling noise continues, this time from the kitten cage. Mr Biscuits is incarcerated again.

VALERIE *is sitting at the kitchen table, nursing a cup of coffee and staring into space.*

DAISY *enters, wearing her pyjama bottoms, big furry slippers and a dressing gown. She's carrying a large Christmas cake – royal icing, silver baubles, etc., and a massive knife.*

VALERIE *is startled.*

VALERIE. Oh!

DAISY. Cake.

VALERIE (*relieved*). Ah. Happy Christmas, Daisy-bell.

DAISY *puts the cake down on the table and stares at it in a very intense way. Stands poised with the knife.*

DAISY (*brisk*). Happy Christmas.

VALERIE. How are you feeling?

DAISY (*brisk, not looking up*). Festive. I thought it might be nice to have the cake for breakfast. It's important not to postpone pleasure unnecessarily.

VALERIE. Absolutely.

DAISY. Seeing as any of us could get hit by a bus at any moment. So I thought I'd cut this up into portions. There are six of us, which means we need eighteen portions. That way we can each have a piece for breakfast, and a piece after lunch with presents, and a piece late this evening if we fancy cake instead of proper dinner.

VALERIE. That sounds… just the job. Well done, Daisy.

DAISY. Thank you. I can see – I can see that my behaviour last night might have caused a certain amount of upset. And whilst I'm not exactly *sorry*, I do feel it's my responsibility to make amends. So I'm organising the cake. I think I'll probably take Mum some cake in bed. I think she'd like that.

VALERIE. Good. Good plan.

DAISY *starts to cut the cake.*

Would you like a coffee?

DAISY. Okay.

VALERIE *gets up and heads over towards the kitchen.*

(*Still slicing the cake.*) I'm wearing my special Christmas T-shirt. Would you like to see it?

VALERIE *stops and turns.*

VALERIE. Yes, that would be lovely.

DAISY *takes off her dressing gown. Underneath it, she's wearing a white T-shirt. It's covered in bloodstains – in the exact same pattern as the bloodstains on Christopher's T-shirt. Only now, they're brown and faded. It's not immediately distinguishable as blood.*

DAISY. Do you like it?

VALERIE. It's – (*Looking at the blood.*) what's that?

DAISY. Blood. It's a replica.

VALERIE. Of what?

DAISY *slices the Christmas cake while she talks to* VALERIE.

DAISY. His one. Christopher's. The one he died in. (*Indicates the brown stains.*) I stabbed myself, last term. I stabbed myself with a pair of scissors, in exactly the same place he got stabbed. So this is probably exactly what his T-shirt looked like. The pattern, I mean. I was going to kill myself and then string myself up on the corkboard so I looked like Jesus on the cross. I'd just got up on the chair to do it when the cleaner walked in.

VALERIE. And that's when you were admitted to the clinic?

DAISY. No. I told her I was rehearsing for a play. The Drama Soc were doing *The Passion* for their end-of-term show. I was admitted to the clinic after I offered to give Professor Barnes a blow job during his eighteenth-century seminar.

VALERIE. Right. Good.

DAISY *is still cutting the Christmas cake. Smaller and smaller pieces.*

DAISY. 'Good.' Interesting. Do you mean good that I wanted to give him a blow job, or good that they stopped me? Because I'm on the fence. I mean, sexuality's nothing to be ashamed of.

VALERIE. Mm.

DAISY. Have you ever –

> DICK *comes in. He's fully dressed, wearing a very natty 'Christmas jumper', and carrying a stocking full of presents.*

DICK. Happy Christmas!

VALERIE. Oh, thank goodness. Would you like a piece of –

> VALERIE *looks at the cake.* DAISY*'s pretty much cut it into crumbs.*

– cake.

DICK. I quite fancy an egg. Does anybody fancy an egg?

DAISY. I'm going to build a snowman.

DICK. But it's not –

VALERIE (*quickly*). Dick.

DICK. No. Yes, you do that. You go and build us all a lovely snowman.

DAISY. I shall. I'll need a coat. It's very cold, isn't it?

VALERIE. Yes, very cold.

> DAISY *goes upstairs.* VALERIE *and* DICK *are alone in the living room.*

DICK. Oh, God. Can we leave now? Please can we leave? We're in over our heads, Val. It's like when the mare gave birth in the back of the lorry at Clacket Lane Services.

VALERIE. We're staying. We're here for them, remember? We follow their lead.

DICK. But they can't want to do Christmas now. It'd be mad.

VALERIE. That's up to them. Have you seen Richard?

> *A brief disturbance as* DAISY *re-enters from upstairs. She's wearing three overcoats and holding a small spade* (*the sort you'd use to shovel coal*). *She heads straight out into the garden.*

DAISY (*on her way out*). Bye!

DICK (*distracted by* DAISY). I think he slept in the shed. Was she wearing my coat?

The front door slams behind DAISY.

VALERIE. You should go out and check on him.

DICK. Not while Daisy's there. She might come at me with the shovel. This is a disaster, Val! This is the worst Christmas ever.

VALERIE. Well, we're all here and we're going to have to make the best of it. We've got the cake, and the tree. And there's ingredients for Christmas dinner. We can cook it together.

DICK. I'm not making my own Christmas dinner!

VALERIE. You may have to.

Pause. VALERIE *and* DICK *are very unhappy.* DICK *gives* VALERIE *the stocking full of presents.*

DICK. I got you this. Just Yardley and chocolate truffles.

VALERIE. Like always.

DICK *smiles.*

DICK. Like always.

VALERIE *takes the stocking and gives* DICK *a kiss.*

VALERIE. Do you think Jennifer's opened hers?

DICK. Is it Christmas there yet? Or has it been and gone? I can never remember.

VALERIE. It's tomorrow there. So she'll be on Boxing Day already.

DICK. Wish we were on Boxing Day already.

VALERIE. We're very lucky though, aren't we?

DICK. What? Why?

VALERIE. That Jennifer turned out how she turned out.

DICK. Really?

VALERIE. Oh, come on.

> LIZZY *comes in from upstairs. She's dressed, and carrying her suitcase in one hand, mobile phone in the other.*

LIZZY. Morning.

VALERIE. Hello. Happy Christmas.

LIZZY. Happy Christmas. Um – did you know that Daisy's in the garden? I saw her through the window. Is she okay?

DICK. I'm surprised you care.

LIZZY. Of course I care.

VALERIE. Yes, she went to build a – she went for a walk.

LIZZY. Well, she's digging up the flowerbed.

DICK. And wearing my overcoat.

VALERIE. Oh. Maybe she's… doing some gardening.

LIZZY. Have either of you got mobile reception? Mine's crap.

DICK. No. Nothing for miles here, I'm afraid. Who are you phoning?

LIZZY. I want to leave. I'm trying to call a cab.

DICK. You'll be lucky.

LIZZY. What? They can't still be pissed.

DICK. Christmas Day. No one works on Christmas Day.

LIZZY. Could one of you please drive me to the station?

DICK. No trains.

LIZZY. Fuck.

> LIZZY *sits down at the table. Put her head in her hands.*

VALERIE. There's cake. Would you like some cake? Or some coffee.

LIZZY. I just want to go home.

DICK. I'm sure no one blames you for last night, if that's what you're worried about. It was her, you know – (*Makes a 'mad' gesture.*) Mad Mabel.

VALERIE. Exactly. Well, no – anyway. You're very welcome here, Lizzy. Don't let anyone make you think otherwise.

RICHARD *blasts in from the shed. He's dressed. Pyjama trousers underneath a tatty red jumper – a concession to Christmas.*

RICHARD. Good morning good morning! A very Merry Christmas, one and all!

VALERIE (*to* LIZZY). You see?

RICHARD. Good morning, Elizabeth. So glad you didn't die in the night.

LIZZY. Oh, for God's sake.

RICHARD *heads straight for the drinks cabinet and pours himself a Scotch.*

VALERIE *and* DICK *can't help but stare.*

VALERIE. Would you like some coffee, Richard?

RICHARD. Not on Christmas morning. That'd be perverse. Christmas morning's for booze, it's the rules. (*Points at* VALERIE*'s coffee.*) For every sip you take of that, a Little Baby Jesus dies.

DICK. Maybe I should do a jug of Buck's Fizz.

RICHARD. Yes, you do that, Dick. You do that. That'll make everything wonderful again.

VALERIE. Have you seen Sally?

RICHARD. No. I have seen Daisy though. She appears to be digging up the Christopher Llewellyn Memorial Flowerbed.

She's doing quite the job. If she goes much deeper she's going to end up joining your daughter in Australia.

VALERIE. Oh, God. Maybe one of us should go and / stop her.

DICK. Bagsy not me.

RICHARD. Leave it. She's got 'Lynda' at the end of the phone for when it all comes crumbling down. She's fine. Ooh, cake.

RICHARD *sits down in front of the cake. Eats a fistful.*

VALERIE. Perhaps I should wake Sally up.

RICHARD. Be my guest.

VALERIE *goes upstairs.* RICHARD *shovels cake into his mouth, as* LIZZY *and* DICK *look on. It's a bit disgusting.*

The kitten mewls from his cage.

DICK. Has he been fed?

RICHARD. I very much doubt it.

DICK *takes a few crumbs of cake from the plate, and nervously pushes it through the bars of the kitten's cage. The kitten lets out a mewl and a hiss.* DICK *snatches his hand back, alarmed.*

DICK. Whoa.

RICHARD. I know. I think he might grow up to be a minotaur.

DICK *peers into the cage.*

DICK. He's got very close-set eyes, hasn't he? Nasty eyes.

The kitten hisses at DICK *from the cage.* DICK *presses his face up close to cage door, and hisses back.*

I'm not afraid of you.

VALERIE *runs in from upstairs, alarmed.*

VALERIE. She's gone.

RICHARD. What?

VALERIE. Sally. She's not there. She's gone.

RICHARD. Where?

VALERIE. I don't know. Should we call the police?

RICHARD. And say what? 'Middle-aged woman not in bed at nine a.m.?'

DICK. Is her car here?

VALERIE *looks out of the window.*

VALERIE. Yes. Still here.

DICK. Well she must be here then.

LIZZY. She sure as hell won't have gone anywhere in a taxi.

VALERIE. Well, she's not in our room, and she's not in her room, and she's not in the bathroom or the kitchen.

RICHARD. Airing cupboard?

VALERIE. Do you think this is funny, Richard?

RICHARD. No. But I do think she's a free woman, and if she wants to go randomly wandering off in the middle of the night then that's her prerogative. Also, none of our business.

VALERIE. That's rubbish and you know it. It's Christmas morning! She hasn't missed a Christmas morning since – for ever. Apart from last year when you were all –

RICHARD. – in a heap on the floor.

VALERIE. – in turmoil. This – this isn't right.

DICK. Did she leave a note?

VALERIE. God, you don't think she's – ?

DICK. No, of course not.

VALERIE. Not Sally. She'd never – I'm going to phone her.

DICK. I'll go and have a root around.

DICK *goes upstairs.*

VALERIE *goes over to the landline – a cordless phone – and dials. Waits for an answer. The kitten mewls from his cage.*

VALERIE (*into phone*). Hello, Sally, it's Valerie. Um – we're all here, and we were wondering where you were. Of course if you've just gone into the garden or something then I'm going to feel awfully silly, especially if you walk in while I'm leaving this message. But – no – you haven't. Anyway. We're a bit worried. Not very worried. Just – well, you know. And there's cake. Could you give us a ring on the landline? Lots of love. Oh, and Happy Christmas. Bye.

VALERIE *hangs up the phone.*

What should we do? Should I put the turkey in?

DAISY *re-enters from the garden, carrying her spade, still wearing three overcoats. She's also carrying one of* SALLY*'s Christmas Crocs.*

DAISY. I've got rid of the Christopher flowerbed. I don't think he likes it, so I've got rid of it. I thought that could be my Christmas present to him. And while I was doing it I found this –

DAISY *holds up the shoe.*

It's Mum's. She must have gone out to look at the flowerbed in the middle of the night.

VALERIE. Just the one shoe?

DAISY. Yes. We should give it back to her, I think. What?

VALERIE. Daisy, darling, your mum's not here. She's gone missing.

DAISY. What?

VALERIE. Well, we don't know for sure she's gone missing.

RICHARD. No one's checked the airing cupboard yet.

DICK *comes in from upstairs, holding a piece of tissue with some writing on it.*

DICK. I found this on her – what's it called. Eiderdown. Counterpane. No, not counterpane. Sort of like a throw, but –

VALERIE. Dick.

VALERIE *snatches the note*.

(*Reading*.) It says 'BOLLOCKS TO THE LOT OF YOU.' In capital letters.

RICHARD. No Sylvia Plath, is she?

DAISY (*frightened*). Mum?

VALERIE. Okay. She's not in her bed, and she's not in any of the other rooms in the house. And she's not in the shed, is she, Richard?

RICHARD. Better not be. That's my shed.

VALERIE. But we've left a message on her phone, and we're certain she'll be back before too long.

DAISY. What? Mum? But –

DAISY *starts to cry*.

VALERIE. Oh no – no – Daisy – don't worry. Please. I'm sure we'll find her. She won't have gone far, she can't have –

DAISY. This isn't Christmas! This isn't what Christmas is supposed to be like!

VALERIE. I know, darling, I know –

DAISY. We should be opening stockings and having scrambled eggs and – nothing works! Nothing – I made Mum run away! I made her –

DAISY *sits down roughly on the sofa, crying*.

VALERIE *goes over to her, puts an arm round her*.

VALERIE. Shh, it's all right. You didn't make her run away.

RICHARD. You bloody did.

VALERIE. She'll be back. We'll find her. We'll find her, and we'll have a lovely day. Don't you worry.

LIZZY, RICHARD and DICK stare at VALERIE and DAISY.

Dick, could you put the turkey in, please?

DICK. What?

VALERIE gives him a look – raised eyebrows.

Right.

VALERIE. It's soaking in orange juice in a bucket in the corner.

RICHARD. Organic orange juice.

DICK. Right.

DICK goes off to put the turkey in.

Scene Three

Living room.

It's a bit later. DICK, RICHARD, DAISY and LIZZY are sitting around, and clearly have been for a while. There are drinks scattered about the place – coffee cups, a jug of Buck's Fizz and a few glasses. Also the Christmas cake, mince pies and plates, some used, some not. RICHARD's drinking Scotch. DICK's drinking Buck's Fizz.

A tortured waiting-room vibe.

DICK. Did you know that what we refer to as Buck's Fizz, isn't actually Buck's Fizz at all? The actual recipe for the drink 'Buck's Fizz' is known only to the barmen of Buck's Club in Mayfair.

No response. DICK examines his drink, holds it up to the light.

Mmm. I think what I'm drinking now is probably technically a Mimosa.

Still no response. DICK *downs his drink.*

Funny old world.

Long pause.

DAISY *gets up and goes over to the window. Stares out.*

LIZZY (*to* DAISY). Are you okay?

DAISY. One of us has got to watch the window. If she's not in the car, we won't be able to hear her coming back. So we have to watch the window. So that when she walks up the drive we can run out and meet her with presents.

DICK, LIZZY *and* RICHARD *look at each other, concerned.*

We should organise a shift for watching the window. (*Turns to* DICK.) Dick, can you help me do a rota?

DICK. Let's just... play it by ear, eh?

DAISY. I'm going to get some pens and paper so we can organise a rota. I made her go away, so I'm going to make sure she comes back.

DAISY *goes upstairs.*

VALERIE *comes back in from the kitchen, holding an oven timer in one hand and the phone in the other.*

VALERIE. I finally spoke to someone at the police station. They say they can't do anything proper until she's been missing for twenty-four hours. But they were ever so helpful, and they said they'd keep an eye out. They're sympathetic to your family situation –

RICHARD. Oh, how kind. How brilliantly *kind* of them to be sympathetic to our poor, sad little situation. How absolutely marvellous they are.

RICHARD *gets up to pour himself another drink.*

VALERIE. I know you're worried –

RICHARD. Oh, I'm not worried! I'm furious. I'm furious with her for just – *prancing off* and inconveniencing us all like this. It was her idea to stage this fucking awful festive extravaganza. The least she could do was stick it out until the bitter end. When she comes back, I tell you, I'm going to be having some serious words.

VALERIE. Not if I've got anything to do with it.

RICHARD. Well, fortunately, Valerie, you *don't* have anything to do with it. No, she's pranced off because she thinks she can, and that's that.

VALERIE. You don't think that your behaviour might have had something to do with it?

RICHARD. *My* behaviour?

VALERIE. Yes. You weren't exactly a tower of support last night, were you? Knocking back the drinks and making snide comments about the –

RICHARD (*mimicking her*). 'Knocking back the drinks and making snide comments about the meh-meh-meh.'

VALERIE. – vegetables. There's really no need to be rude, Richard.

RICHARD. Well, I'm sorry. I'm not much in the mood for company. Not until we find out whether or not my dear wife's wandered off into the woods to die.

Pause.

VALERIE. You don't think she's –

RICHARD. Offed herself? No. Not a chance.

DICK. She had one shoe on.

VALERIE. What?

DICK. It's a positive. I mean, there's only so much you can do with one shoe on.

VALERIE turns back to RICHARD.

VALERIE. Richard, I know this is hard. And I know you want to protect yourself from – the worst thoughts. But do you think there's any reasonable grounds to suspect that Sally's harmed herself?

RICHARD *shrugs*.

Has she ever tried to harm herself before, Richard?

Pause. RICHARD *doesn't want to answer.*

RICHARD. Yes. Once. Six months ago. She was about to – when I walked in. But it was a *good* thing, she said. A turning point. She started the Foundation just afterwards.

VALERIE. Right. Okay. Right.

DICK. God.

Pause.

RICHARD. Minibus to Beachy Head then, team? Bit cold for ice creams, but the view'll be smashing.

Everyone stares at RICHARD.

Oh, what? She hasn't done anything stupid. She hasn't. Not Sally, and not at Christmas. It's… impossible. Can we put the idea to bed, please? At least until tomorrow. She'll be back.

Pause.

The kitten mewls from the cage.

DICK. We really should let him out.

VALERIE. We can't. It'll traumatise him.

DICK. If he's got through the last twenty-four hours then I think he can cope with anything.

RICHARD. Just leave him.

They all remain uncomfortably in situ *for a moment.*

DICK. Maybe we should all play a game.

VALERIE. Yes, that might pass the time. Richard, have you got any games?

RICHARD. No. They're all in the attic. We're not much of a 'games' family any more.

VALERIE. There must be something we could play where we won't need an actual / game.

DICK. Wink Murder! (*He doesn't realise what he's said*.)

> LIZZY *chokes on her drink*. DICK *realises what he's said*.

Or Charades.

VALERIE. Perhaps we could watch television. Richard?

> RICHARD *shrugs*. *He doesn't care*.

> VALERIE *turns on the television*. *It's a twenty-four-hour rolling-news channel*. *They're on the Trafalgar Square stabbing*.

REPORTER (*on telly*). 'Back to the young man who was fatally stabbed yesterday in Trafalgar Square. Police are still appealing for witnesses to come forward with any further information on...'

> VALERIE *changes the channel*. *A continuity announcer*.

CONTINUITY ANNOUNCER. '...*a heartwarming treat for all the family* – Chalet Girl...'

> VALERIE *turns off the television*.

VALERIE. Maybe not.

DICK. What time's the Queen?

VALERIE. Not for hours yet.

DICK. We've got to have our turkey before the Queen.

> LIZZY *gets up*. *Goes over to the window*.

LIZZY. For fuck's sake.

DICK. What?

LIZZY. You! With your turkey and your Buck's Fizz and your Queen! What's wrong with you?

RICHARD. Nothing. This is how we operate.

LIZZY. Well, it's a treat, isn't it? This is just a *box of delights* –

RICHARD. You're the one who caused all this! We were having a lovely Christmas before –

LIZZY. Oh yes, lovely –

RICHARD. – you opened your big fat gob.

LIZZY (*completely furious*). What? Oh, I'm sorry. What was I supposed to do? With you shouting in one ear and your mentally ill daughter all but shoving a fork in my throat? Keep schtum? Stiff upper lip? Pull a cracker, compliment the gravy?

RICHARD. Yes! Why not? And Daisy's not mentally ill! She just needs to man up a bit.

LIZZY. Like you? Mm, you're quite the hero. Indispensible. Out in the shed, staring at the walls, swigging from a bottle of Domestos and gnawing on a brick.

DICK *laughs*.

DICK. That's actually quite a funny im/age.

VALERIE. Dick, be quiet.

DICK. What? For God's sake, it's Christmas. Can't we have a joke?

LIZZY *speaks to* RICHARD.

LIZZY. Look, I know I agreed to come and – play along with Sally's Christmas. I did it because I thought it would be kind. But that's all gone now, and you need to deal with it. Deal with the new situation.

RICHARD (*furious*). I've been fucking dealing with it for the last year! And where've you been all that time? Off living your life. Forgetting about us. Not answering Sally's calls.

LIZZY *looks away, hurt.* RICHARD *persists.*

You know, Christopher never touched drugs before he met you. It was your fault. You broke him.

LIZZY *turns on* RICHARD.

LIZZY. That's bullshit! That is *total* bullshit and you know it is –

VALERIE *steps in.*

VALERIE. Enough! This isn't helping. We all need to… pull together.

LIZZY. No! He needs to hear this. (*Back to* RICHARD.) Your wife's gone missing. Your daughter's gone nuts. Your junkie, dealer son's been murdered –

RICHARD *stands up, roars.*

RICHARD. *How dare you!*

LIZZY *squares up to him, shouts back.*

LIZZY. Don't you shout at me, you pissed old fuck! And I'll call him a junkie if I want, because that's what he was. Everyone knows it now, it's all out, might as well use the right words. And you don't give a shit. You're a ruin. You're a dried-up old ruin of a man.

RICHARD *looks as if he's about to take a swing at* LIZZY. DICK *grabs his arm.*

DICK. Whoa.

VALERIE. Lizzy! There's no need for that.

LIZZY *ignores her. Carries on addressing* RICHARD, *intense.*

LIZZY. Do you remember what you used to be like? Remember when I came to stay for the summer, ten years ago? You'd just given up drinking. It was great, you were over the moon. And one day I was a bit quiet, and you realised it was because it was my birthday and no one knew and I didn't have any presents. And you'd heard I liked Scalextrics, so you drove two hours to Toys R Us to get me some. And you lied about it because you didn't want me to know how much trouble you'd gone to. You said you'd had it in the garage, just found it! Brand-new Scalextrics. Do you remember that? It was the nicest thing anyone's ever done for me. And you did it.

A beat. RICHARD *and* LIZZY *look at each other.*

And now – just fucking look at you. Look, I loved your son, and I'm sorry for your loss. But this is not my fault, and I will not be blamed for it. (*Pause.*) The ball's in your court now, Richard.

RICHARD *slams down his drink, and storms out, slamming the door behind him.*

DICK *exhales. That was a bit dramatic.*

LIZZY *sits down, shaken.*

VALERIE. That was brave of you. And it needed to be said.

LIZZY. Thanks.

VALERIE (*gently*). Why did you come here, Lizzy?

LIZZY *shrugs.*

LIZZY. Sally invited me. And invited me and invited me and invited me.

VALERIE *smiles a bit at this.* LIZZY *continues.*

And Christopher always used to go on about Christmas here, and how it was special. He looked like a little kid when he talked about it, sometimes. He got excited in November. It was mental. So I thought I might come and see what all the fuss was about. (*Near to tears.*) And now I feel like I've just ruined it.

Silence. No one speaks.

VALERIE. Look – Sally invited you here because she wanted, as she put it, 'a little slice of Christopher'. And you've absolutely given us that.

*LIZZY gives VALERIE a bit of a 'you're kidding, right?'
look.*

You have! Yes, things went… odd. But we were able to talk
about the good times, weren't we? And the bad times don't
cancel out the good times.

LIZZY. No. No, I suppose not.

DICK. How about another Buck's Fizz? Pass the time.

LIZZY. Yes, why not?

DICK. I'll whizz up a fresh jug.

The oven timer goes off in the kitchen.

VALERIE. Turkey needs basting. Dick, can you help me
wrangle the bird?

VALERIE and DICK go off into the kitchen.

LIZZY. I need a fag.

LIZZY goes outside.

The room's empty for a moment.

We can hear someone coming down the stairs.

DAISY (*offstage*). I've given up on the rota, as there's only five
of us. But I went up in the attic and I found –

*DAISY comes in from upstairs. She's carrying a boxed toy –
the Penguin Race.*

Oh.

*DAISY puts the Penguin Race carefully on the table. She
opens the box, and takes out the toy. It's a plastic slide (sort
of like a water flume or a bobsled track) and some little
plastic penguins.*

*DAISY lines the three penguins up on the table in front of
her.*

She addresses the penguins, like a coach before the big race.

Now, we're going to keep this clean. Good clean race.
What's going to happen is this. I'm going to set you off, then
when the first of you gets to the top I'm going to run round
the table. If I get round the table before you reach the
bottom, then I win. If you reach the bottom before I get
round the table, then I win. Okay?

DAISY *looks at the penguins.*

Don't give me any of that. I have very good reasons for
wanting to do this. Okay? Good. Then we're off.

DAISY *puts the penguins in their starting positions, and
turns the toy on. It makes a chirping noise, as the penguins
are mechanically conveyed to the top of the slide.*

DAISY *keeps a firm eye on the penguins, as she gets into a
sprinter's starting position.*

One – two – three – *three – THREE –*

*The penguins have got jammed at the top of the slide. Bit of a
pile-up.*

Fuck!

The door from outside opens. LIZZY *comes in.*

LIZZY. What are you –

DAISY *panics, and tries to hide the toy. Fails (it's quite big).*

DAISY. Nothing! Fuck off! Fuck off!

LIZZY. Sorry. I didn't mean to –

DAISY. It's fine.

LIZZY. Are you okay?

DAISY. Yes. Absolutely fine.

LIZZY *looks at the toy.*

LIZZY. Is that the Penguin Race?

DAISY (*hostile*). What's it to you?

LIZZY. Sorry. None of my business.

DAISY. How do you know about the Penguin Race? (*Pause*.) Did he tell you about it?

LIZZY *nods*.

What did he say?

LIZZY. Nothing much – just – we were talking about toys. I said, I hadn't really grown up with toys. So he told me about some of his. He said he wished he could give me his old toys.

DAISY. Well, you're not having / this.

LIZZY. I wasn't asking for it.

Pause. DAISY *sits down in the front of the Penguin Race, and plays with it.*

DAISY. Has anyone heard from Mum?

LIZZY. No. But they've put the turkey on. Not that that's going to make her come back, but –

DAISY. It means people think she's going to come back.

LIZZY *nods*.

I don't think she's going to come back. I think she's probably dead. I think I probably killed her.

LIZZY *looks at* DAISY, *shocked.* DAISY *shrugs*.

I've been told that I have to be honest about what I feel about things. And that's what I feel about that.

LIZZY. Oh.

DAISY. It's important to be honest.

LIZZY. Yep.

DAISY. But sometimes I can be too honest. Like when I walked in yesterday and saw you here and said 'Oh fuck, it's you.' I shouldn't have been rude to you. I reacted, rather than responded, and I'm sorry about that.

LIZZY. That's okay.

Pause.

DAISY. If I'd *responded* – if I'd really gone through my communications toolbox and selected the most appropriate and compassionate words, I would have said something like, 'Oh, it's you, I wasn't expecting you to be here, and I'm not entirely sure I'm happy about it.'

LIZZY. Right.

DAISY. And then later, when I was trying to make you tell the truth at dinner, it occurs to me that I could have gone about it in a different way. Like, I could have taken you aside beforehand and suggested that we gently bring up the truth about Christopher, acknowledging our own needs, whilst respecting Mum's. I could have done that. But I was too angry.

LIZZY. Okay.

DAISY. I couldn't believe you'd come. I mean – you. Of all people. If you'd come to – blow the whole thing apart. Bust it all open. Spread a few home truths, then I could've gone along with that. But you just rocked up and played Mum's game. Which I hated.

LIZZY. I know.

DAISY. I don't hate *you*, you know.

LIZZY. Yes, you do.

DAISY. No. I never said I hated you. I said that I blamed you for Christopher's death, and that obviously coloured the way I felt about you. But I've spent some time re-examining my feelings –

LIZZY. Oh God.

DAISY. – and I'm coming to the conclusion that whilst you *are* someone I associate with his killing, I'm not in possession of all the facts. So perhaps my feelings aren't rooted in the truth.

LIZZY. Oh.

DAISY. I haven't quite figured it all out yet. I've still got to complete a workbook on you, and I imagine that Lynda will have some things to say.

LIZZY. Oh. Well, do... do get back to me on that.

DAISY. I probably won't. It's unlikely that we'll ever have an enjoyable relationship.

LIZZY. Yep. Great.

DAISY. I did do a psycho-drama exercise on you, though. Just last week. It was fun.

LIZZY. Oh?

DAISY. Yes. I called you my 'Guilt Sister'. And I did a drawing of you, which was a drawing of a spider with a beard.

LIZZY. Beard?

DAISY. That was me being playful. The beard was just for fun. The 'sister' bit comes from you staying here in the summer holidays, then you getting together with Christopher, which made you even more of a sister. The 'guilt' bit's more fiddly –

LIZZY. You know, you really don't have to tell me this.

DAISY. I want to. It's important for me to be open. I feel guilty around you because you were born with less than I was born with, and because you're from Peckham. Which is just middle-class guilt, I suppose. Slightly less comfortably, I feel guilty around you because you're black. I've not examined this yet, but I have a hunch that it somehow dates back to the slaves. You know, white guilt.

LIZZY. White guilt.

DAISY. Mm. It's more common that you'd think. Mum's definitely got it. Dad doesn't have it, but that's probably because he's too drunk to feel anything at all. *Then* – and here's where it gets interesting – I may be projecting some of *my own* guilt about Christopher's death onto you.

LIZZY. You feel guilty.

DAISY. Absolutely. Survivor guilt. Not-being-there guilt. Guilt at my own basic powerlessness over fate and things, which is daft because we're all powerless. Guilt over his taking lots of drugs, and his buying them from non-posh, non-white people, which fed into the cycle of violence which kills hundreds of people all over the world on a daily basis, and which ultimately killed him. Which is reflected in my own *internal* cycle of violence, which is what led to my incident. It's all very complicated.

LIZZY. Yikes. That's… quite some therapising.

DAISY. Well, it's what you get given if you're middle-class and you stab yourself with scissors. (*Brief pause.*) I'm hot.

DAISY *sits down at the table, and takes off her hoodie. She's wearing the bloodstained T-shirt.* LIZZY *looks at it, shocked.*

LIZZY. Is that blood?

DAISY. Yep. I wear it a lot. I wear it when I want to remember how we all got into this state.

Pause. DAISY *plays with the Penguin Race a bit more.* LIZZY *watches her.*

LIZZY. I shouted at your dad. Just now.

DAISY. Good. He needs shouting at.

Pause.

LIZZY. I think you really offended Dick last night.

DAISY. I know. Poor old Dick. I shouldn't have done that. That was cheeky of me.

The ghost of a smile on DAISY*'s face.*

LIZZY. Do you think he's really all right with his daughter? The baby thing.

DAISY. He will be. Valerie makes him read the *Guardian*.
Every morning, cover to cover. She stands over him and
points out the articles he might like to learn something from.

LIZZY *smiles*.

LIZZY. I like you, Daisy. I really do. I always have. You were
fun.

DAISY. That's nice.

LIZZY. And I didn't come here to hurt you. I came here because
your mum asked me three times, and I didn't know how to
say no.

DAISY. She was lying. And you joined in with her lie. That
wasn't helping her.

LIZZY. Sometimes you have to face up to the truth bit by bit.
Because it hurts too much to see it all at once.

Pause.

DAISY. Did you really love him?

LIZZY. What?

DAISY. Christopher.

LIZZY. Yes. For a while. Yes, I did. I loved you all. I still do.

DAISY. Are you sorry he's dead?

LIZZY (*pause, speaks quietly, sincere*). Yes.

DAISY. Then why didn't you come to the funeral?

LIZZY. I couldn't.

DAISY. Lots of people had work, and they took the day off.
People who didn't even like him very much, let alone love
him. They still came.

LIZZY. It was complicated.

DAISY. How?

LIZZY. I don't know. I've not figured it all out. I've not got a
Lynda.

DAISY. Poor you.

LIZZY. I thought that seeing you lot might help me figure it out.

Pause.

DAISY. I spoke at the funeral.

LIZZY. I heard. I heard you were great.

DAISY. Some people thought so. Some people didn't. I was...
controversial, not that I regret that. You know, I thought that
that was going to be the hardest thing I'd ever have to do.
But it wasn't. That was the easy bit. That was the fucking
shallow end. It's all been downhill since then.

LIZZY. I know.

DAISY. And all the pretending's made it harder. That's why I
went mad. I couldn't handle the pretending any more.

LIZZY *looks hard at* DAISY.

LIZZY. I don't think you're mad at all, you know. I think you're
just really sad. And angry. And you want people to see it, but
they won't. So you're having to –

DAISY *interrupts her, sharply.*

DAISY. Lynda thinks I'm bipolar. Or maybe that I have
borderline personality disorder. She's going to tell me when I
go back.

LIZZY. Okay.

DAISY *starts to breathe very heavily. Puts her head in her
hands on the table.*

Are you all right?

DAISY*'s suddenly really panicked.*

DAISY. Do you think my mum's killed herself? I've got this
feeling. It's the feeling I had – or I remember having had –
just before I got the call to say that Christopher had died. It's
as if my chest's caving in, and everything's pulsing at me
and –

LIZZY *goes over to her and sits her down. Pours her the nearest available drink – a Buck's Fizz.*

LIZZY. Sit down. It's just a panic attack. It'll pass.

DAISY. No, it's not, it's all getting louder – she's dead – she's dead and she's alone, I know she is – she's – there's no way that anything's going to be okay – there's no way –

LIZZY. It's okay. It's a panic attack. It's a panic attack.

Now LIZZY*'s panicking a bit.*

DAISY. I can see spots – she's dead, I know she's dead – we're going to hear she's dead / – everything's over –

LIZZY. It's a panic attack, it's all in your head, it's –

The phone rings. DAISY *starts to scream. And scream and scream and scream.*

VALERIE *runs in from the kitchen.* LIZZY *shouts at them, whilst putting a hand over* DAISY*'s mouth.*

The phone! Answer the phone!

VALERIE *answers the phone.*

VALERIE (*into phone*). Hello?

Sirens, flashing lights, newsreaders and reporters– 'armed police,' 'multiple stab wounds,' 'Christmas revellers,' 'unfathomable violence,' 'otherwise peaceful Christmas,' 'deprivation and decay,' 'mounting tensions,' 'multiple stab wounds,' 'witnesses' and round and round and round.

End of Act Two.

ACT THREE

Scene One

RICHARD*'s shed.*

A bit later – dusk. RICHARD*'s in his shed. He's got two empty wine bottles beside him, and a glass of Scotch on the go.*

He's in the armchair. The shed's messier than before. He's opened a couple of the boxes – Christopher's things, it turns out. He's looking at some school photos – smart portraits of Christopher in school uniform. RICHARD*'s got a cricket bat on his lap.*

He'd like to be crying, but he isn't. He's just glassy, sixty-percent drunk.

A knock on the door of the shed.

RICHARD. Yep.

The door opens – it's DICK. DICK *comes in, and closes the door behind him. Stands awkwardly over* RICHARD. *Clocks the empty bottles and the tumbler of Scotch.*

DICK. Hello.

RICHARD *raises his glass to* DICK *by way of a greeting.*

RICHARD. Am I in disgrace?

DICK. No. No more so than usual.

RICHARD *bounces the cricket bat in his hand for a moment. Stares at it.*

Valerie was wondering if you'd like to come back into the house. There's turkey.

RICHARD. I don't want turkey.

DICK. She says you have to have it, or you'll pass out.

RICHARD. Does she?

DICK. You should come in the house, Richard. It's better in the house.

RICHARD. There's nothing for me there.

DICK. We've got the cat out. He's all right. We quite like him now.

RICHARD *stares into his glass.*

RICHARD. Nothing for me in this world. Nothing.

DICK. Oh, come on! You've got… lots. You've got your shed. You've got –

RICHARD. Everyone hates me in there, Dick. Lizzy, Daisy, Valerie, the fucking cat. They think I'm just some… stupid angry lush.

DICK. No… surely not.

RICHARD. Lizzy's right. I am just a pissed old fuck. And Sally's offed herself –

DICK. We don't know that.

RICHARD. I do. It's been months coming. I just – ignored it. I'm a terrible husband, terrible father, terrible man. I'm just a Scotch-sodden bag of meat. (*Pause.*) I might as well have killed her with my bare hands, Dick.

DICK. No. No. Don't say that. If anyone did it was Dai– well, no. It's no one's fault. Nothing's anyone's fault. We're all doing our best.

RICHARD *takes a swig of his whisky.*

RICHARD. I've thought about doing it myself, you know. Made a few plans. Noose, knife, bleach. Fall on my sword like a soldier. Has to be done, sometimes. Some people, not meant to live.

DICK. No. Don't you dare. Don't even think it.

RICHARD *puts his head in his hands.*

RICHARD. I'm fucked. Everything's fucked.

DICK. Oh, come on! It's Christmas Day. That's got to be worth
something.

RICHARD. Christmas Day is fucked.

DICK. There's still a few hours to go.

RICHARD. Every day's fucked! Friday – it happened on
Friday. So every Friday I wake up and think, here we are
again, going over it all again. Saturday – that was when we
went to see the undertaker. Sunday – Daisy came home.
Monday – police say they can't release the body. Tuesday –
Sally, all day, throwing up and shaking. Wednesday – back
on the drink, properly on the drink. Then before you know it
it's Friday again, round and round and – (*Stops, choked.*)

Pause.

DICK (*tentatively*). Thursday?

RICHARD (*quickly*). No, that's fucked as well. Everyone hates
Thursdays.

DICK *doesn't know what to say.*

I dream about it. Every night. That day. Police tape. Tent. I
came straight from work. Ran from the office. They ordered
a car, but I couldn't wait. Needed to run. Over the bridge,
down by the river. Party boats, joggers. I knew the way.
Don't know how I knew the way. Just veered off, crossed
three streets, and there it all was.

They wouldn't let me see him. Wouldn't let me in the tent.
Bit of blood trickling out the bottom – it was sort of on a
slope. People keeping people back. Crime scene. I knew they
were just doing their jobs. Made it worse, actually. Another
day at the office. I just *stood* there, Dick, feeling as if I was
in the way. You think you should be crying, you know?
Gnashing at the pavement like on *Casualty*. But no – just
stood there. Thinking – this isn't my world. This isn't one of
the places I go. I shouldn't be here.

My phone rang. Bloody embarrassing – everyone looked. It was James, my friend from – from being sober. Don't know how he knew to call. I didn't answer. Wish I'd answered.

Every night I dream about it. Tent, tape, blood. Or some version of it. Too many bad dreams. Gone on for too long.

DICK. It's not been that long, really.

RICHARD *shakes his head.*

RICHARD. Too long. Too long. So, I drink.

DICK. Does drinking make the dreams better?

RICHARD. More violent, less distinct. Less distinct is better.

DICK. You could knock it on the head, Richard. The drinking. You did before – it was –

RICHARD. Nine years. Not a drop.

DICK. Well, you've done it before, you can do it again! Go back to those people who helped you, in the church hall. James, that lot. They were nice.

RICHARD. Yes, they were.

DICK. So…

RICHARD *shakes his head.*

RICHARD. No. No happy endings. Not this time. We're too far gone.

Pause. RICHARD *finishes his drink.*

He was a good boy.

DICK. I know he was.

RICHARD. We did all we could, Dick. They were fed, clothed, schooled, loved. Never abused, never afraid, never ignored. And then… this.

DICK. Yes, but they grow up, you know? Become their own people. I mean, Jennifer. I might huff and puff about it a bit – but it's just *her*. You know? I'm not putting this very well. I suppose what I'm trying to say is that while you think they're your children, and everything's down to you, sometimes they just do things which leave you so totally flummoxed that you wonder if there was a mix-up in the maternity ward. And then you realise that that's because they're not you, they're them. And that's that. You see?

RICHARD. Hmm.

Pause. RICHARD *stares at the floor. Exhales.*

Is life just a terrible process of attrition? You're born with joy and then it's hacked away and away and away until all you can do is curl up and moan through the fist-crushing agony of it all?

DICK *thinks for a moment.*

DICK. Well – maybe.

RICHARD. Brilliant.

DICK. But you've got to keep on, Richard! Just bugger on through it. Chop wood, carry water. You can't keep going all… Greek, every time things get rough.

RICHARD. It's unbearable.

DICK. Yes, it is! But that doesn't mean there's no fun to be had. Look, I'm not an alcohol therapist or a social worker or a private-psychiatric-clinic doctor, but I am a person. I've been a person for fifty-two years. So I know that people are resilient. Disgustingly so.

RICHARD. Mm.

DICK. Unless they choose not to be.

Pause.

RICHARD. Mm.

DICK. Come and meet the cat. He really is great. There's talk of us putting a hat on him for a laugh.

RICHARD *stares into his glass.*

A knock on the door of the shed.

Hello?

It's DAISY. *She seems excited. Happy.*

DAISY. Dad! Dick! Mum's back! AND – there's been a Christmas miracle!

RICHARD. All right, Daisy. We'll be with you in a moment.

DAISY *runs off.*

DICK *turns back to* RICHARD.

DICK. Richard? In the market for a Christmas miracle?

RICHARD. Oh, all right.

Scene Two

Living room.

Still the same mess of plates and glasses as there was before, but now there's a bit more of it. Bottle of wine on the go – some plates and knives and forks. Also, a few carrier bags, full of food.

The Penguin Race is set up again, this time on the sideboard.

SALLY*'s sitting at the table – she's the centre of attention. She's wearing a white nightdress with a coat slung over it. She looks a bit dazed, but not unhappy.*

VALERIE *pours a glass of wine, puts it in front of* SALLY.

VALERIE. There you go.

SALLY. Oh, thank you.

SALLY *takes a sip of her wine.*

DAISY *is holding the kitten out of his cage.*

DAISY. And here's Mr Biscuits.

SALLY *takes the kitten. Looks at him, enchanted.*

SALLY. He's quite the little thing, isn't he? Hello, kitten-cat.
Happy Christmas.

SALLY *tickles the top of his head. Talks to the kitten.*

We should have let you out before, shouldn't we? I think
you'd have been able to handle it. You're tough as old boots,
aren't you, Mr Biscuits? I can tell.

VALERIE *takes her glass of wine, and sits down with*
SALLY.

VALERIE. Okay, so you got up –

SALLY. Yes. And it was the strangest thing. I felt so so
miserable. I don't think I've ever felt so miserable. Well,
maybe apart from –

VALERIE. Yes.

SALLY. – yes. And the time when I tried to –

VALERIE. Yes.

SALLY. Anyway, I felt dreadful. So I got up to put the turkey
in, and then thought 'I don't want to put the bloody turkey
in. I don't even like turkey. I just want to do something –
something absolutely atrocious. Something absolutely
horribly shocking.' So I ate half the yule log –

VALERIE. Oh, I thought that must've been Dick.

SALLY. No, it was me. I ate it with my hands at five o'clock in
the morning, ha! And then I went to look at Christopher's
flowerbed. And somewhere between the sugar rush and
terrible pain of it all I started walking. And walking and
walking and walking. And I was having an argument in my
head, about Christmas, and Christopher, and *why the hell* do
I have to be good? Why do I have to keep everything
together? Why do I have to be tidy and upfront and nice and
kind and run the Foundation and chop the sprouts and make
sure Richard doesn't drink too much and light the candles
and read the poem and –

VALERIE. Yes.

SALLY. – lay the table and sort the presents and commission the poetry and keep all the secrets and make everything lovely? Why? I don't want to do that any more. I want to be bad. Anyway, before I knew it I'd reached the twenty-four-hour garage on the Maldeston roundabout. You know, the one with the little shop.

VALERIE. That's eight miles away.

SALLY. I know! I was like Forrest Gump. Anyway, there I was, and it was open. So I wandered in and thought – maybe I should get something lovely to make Christmas perfect, to say sorry for running away. And then I thought 'No, Sally, *no!* Christmas isn't perfect! You can't give Christopher one last Christmas, because he's dead, he's dead as a doornail! Ha ha!' So I took a basket and filled it with – (*Gestures to the bag on the table.*) well, all this crap.

LIZZY *peers into the bag.*

LIZZY. Arctic roll. Findus Crispy Pancakes. Ginsters.

SALLY. I thought – let's be disgusting. If we can't have the Christmas I want, let's do *bad* Christmas dinner. Crack-house Christmas.

LIZZY. I love Arctic roll.

DAISY. Me too.

SALLY. And I didn't have my wallet, of course, because I was in my nightie with one shoe on, ha! But it didn't matter as by the time I'd got to the checkout someone had pressed the alarm thing. Anyway, I had a little cry, and a chat to the nice cashier – he was so *tiny*, just a boy, only twenty-one – and it turned out that the he'd been at primary school with Christopher, so he gave me all of these lovely things for free. Bagged them up and everything. And then the nice policemen drove me home. They told me to say Happy Christmas to you all.

VALERIE. What an adventure you've had.

SALLY. Do you know, I really have. In the oddest way, I've had a wonderful day. I've had exactly the day I needed to have.

VALERIE. Well, we're all very pleased to have you back.

SALLY. How is everyone? Is everyone all right?

DAISY. We're all fine! We're all together, and Dad's coming in from the shed –

SALLY *turns to* VALERIE.

SALLY. Is he? Is Richard coming in for dinner?

VALERIE. I hope so.

DAISY. – and we're all going to be together on Christmas Day! And and *and* –

RICHARD *and* DICK *come from outside.*

DICK. The wandering heroes have returned.

RICHARD. Hello, Sally. Happy Christmas.

SALLY. Happy Christmas.

RICHARD. What's this miracle then, Daisy?

DAISY *runs over to the Penguin Race.*

DAISY. Look! (*Turns it on – it's working perfectly; the penguins trot up to the top, then move smoothly down the slide.*) It's working! The penguins!

RICHARD. Well, I'll be damned.

DAISY. And Mum went mental in twenty-four-hour garage and bought Arctic roll, and we all like the kitten, and it properly feels like Christmas. Doesn't it? It does, a bit. I think. I mean, it's still basically awful, in a way, but –

RICHARD. We can live with that.

DAISY. Yes.

VALERIE. There'll be a turkey in ten minutes or so. I haven't done anything to go with it. So it'll just be a big dead bird on the table.

DAISY. There's my festive centrepiece. We could put it next to that. And we can have the Arctic roll and the Crispy Pancakes.

VALERIE. Yes, that might be nice. Does anyone need a drink?

DICK glances at RICHARD. RICHARD pauses for a moment, then steps forward.

RICHARD. No. We need to do something Christmassy.

Everyone looks at RICHARD, surprised.

Don't care what. Just something.

DAISY. We could put the star on the tree.

SALLY. Really, Daisy?

DAISY nods.

DAISY. Yes.

SALLY. I worry that your father's not safe to get up on the chair.

DAISY. Lizzy could do it.

LIZZY. Really?

DAISY. Yeah, I wouldn't mind that. I think it would be okay.

RICHARD. Uh – yes. Okay.

DAISY. So?

DAISY reaches behind the photograph of Christopher, and pulls out an old tinsel star. She hands it to LIZZY. LIZZY gets up on a chair and puts the star on the tree.

Everyone watches her.

End.

www.nickhernbooks.co.uk

facebook.com/nickhernbooks

twitter.com/nickhernbooks